Adam Michie is a Product Developer in legal publishing. He is a proud Tottenham Hotspur fan, although he has found room in his heart for Leyton Orient. He can be found on Twitter using @flicksandtricks.

ORIENTATION

ADAM MICHIE

Chequered Flag
PUBLISHING

First published in the UK by Chequered Flag Publishing
PO Box 4669, Sheffield, S6 9ET
www.chequeredflagpublishing.co.uk

A CIP record for this book is available from the British
Library

Printed in the UK by Henry Ling Limited

ISBN 978-0-9569460-1-0

This book is dedicated to my nanna, without whose kindness and generosity I may never have seen any live football at all. You are greatly missed.

Florence Margaret Cronin 1924-2011

Contents

Orientation

o·ri·en·ta·tion

noun

1. The relative position or direction of something; the bearing or lie of a thing.

2. The action or process of ascertaining one's position relative to the points of the compass, or other specified points; the faculty of doing this; awareness of one's bearings or relative position.

3. A person's basic attitude, beliefs, or feelings; a person's emotional or intellectual position in respect of a particular topic, circumstance, etc.

4. A course intended to provide such familiarisation.

Prologue

I've been in love with football for as long as I can remember. It's hard to say exactly when the infatuation began: like learning to walk, the precise epiphinal moment of enlightenment has been lost in the vagaries of time. I have hazy memories of the European Championships in 1988, but those wispy threads of childish recollection may well have been planted by more recent exposure to YouTube and television clips.

If I have to put a date on it, 25th February 1989 seems the logical choice. That particular Saturday afternoon I made the journey from my home town of Billericay in Essex to West Ham United's Upton Park.

My introduction to live football was inauspicious. Nothing suggested that it was the first tentative step into a world that has brought me many moments of disappointment, joy, anger and ecstasy. I was taken by my dad, who despite never actually saying he disliked football, has never held any innate interest in it. Unlike other father-son relationships where the football torch is passed proudly from one to the other, the sum total of football-related interactions with my dad amounted to him quietly leaning on his brolly on the touchline at Sunday League games, standing clumsily on a couple of my Subbuteo men and my begging his forgiveness after I put the kitchen window through with a wayward volley.

The match itself was a forgettable affair. West Ham, rooted to the foot of the First Division and destined for the drop, played out a 0-0 draw with Queens Park Rangers, who were comfortably mid-table with no pretensions of progressing in the league and no threat of relegation.

We sat in the upper tier of the East Stand, front row on the halfway line, overlooking Upton Park's famous Chicken Run. They were 'the best seats in the house' according to my grandad, who had given up his and my nan's tickets for us.

There were a few well-known faces on the field that day. West Ham had a young dynamo called Paul Ince in midfield and an aging but still majestic Liam Brady wearing the number 10 jersey up front. QPR had the 25-year-old hands of David Seaman between the posts and the soon-to-be West Ham legend Martin 'Mad Dog' Allen hareing around their midfield.

All of this passed me by at the time. The intelligent movement of the players, intricate networks of passes and the ebb and flow of the game – the things that more discerning followers of football regard as essential – were entirely lost on me. As a young boy, just two weeks past my sixth birthday, what happened to the men in the claret-and-blue and blue-and-white hoops was second best to something far more inspiring.

There were less than 18,000 people in the stands that day, a drop in the ocean compared to some of the attendances that frequented football before all-seater stadia were introduced. Yet it was still the largest gathering of people I had ever seen. To my right the North Bank terrace (which has since become the Sir Trevor Brooking Stand) was rocking to and fro. The sound of stamping feet echoed around the ground. I tried in vain to join in but my legs hung limply from the seat, unable to reach the floor, let alone stamp on it.

To others of my age, the experience could have been quite intimidating. I meandered through the sea of legs before kick-off, clutching my dad's hand, feeling smaller than I ever had before. Presented with an uneventful game that I knew little about, my early exposure to that smoke-filled stand and roaring crowd could have put me off the sport for life. But, as fate would have it, I felt nothing but excitement, despite not really knowing what everyone else was getting excited about. The shouting, the chanting, the swearing, the smell of tea and cigarettes; it all wove together to create something so intoxicating that twenty-one years later I still crave it.

Yet the football that I experienced that day was approaching apocalypse and that would be all I ever got to see of it. The landscape of the game and the world I had just discovered was about to change irrevocably.

English football was in the doldrums in the late eighties. England had been dumped out of the 1988 European Championships after losing every game. English clubs were banned from European competition after the Heysel Stadium tragedy. The West Ham match I attended in February 1989 was just a matter of weeks before 96 people were crushed to death at Hillsborough Stadium during an FA Cup semi-final between Liverpool and Nottingham Forest.

The Hillsborough tragedy marked a watershed in English football history. Safety became paramount and the terraces that had welcomed families and friends for generations made way for banks of seats. Soon after the Premier League was born, and along with Sky TV, football was injected with more vigour and vitality – and money – than it had ever seen. The razzmatazz that the Premier League and Sky Sports brought to English football was a breath of fresh air. Players from the four corners of the globe flooded into the English game and brought with them a taste of the exotic. Catching a glimpse of stars from the continent was previously confined to international tournaments every two or four years. They were now on our doorsteps, playing for our clubs.

While English football was experiencing its renaissance, my football journey had made its way to north London and White Hart Lane. Despite my early introduction to the claret and blue of West Ham and the best attempts of my grandad to make me adopt the Hammers as my own, the club never truly captured my imagination. He took me to several more games over the intervening years, and although I cheered and despaired in equal measure, it never truly felt like my team. I loved going, of course. The pie and mash, the sweets my grandad would buy me, leafing through the programme, wearing a replica shirt: it all brought me great joy, but even at the age of seven or eight I remember it being not quite what I wanted.

Going to West Ham with my grandad had been great, but I couldn't really be myself with him. I wanted to scream and shout like everyone else but I felt I was supposed to sit quietly and just watch the match. He had been sitting in those seats for years (he still does) and the people in the adjacent seats knew him and my nan well. I'd always sit between him and his mate Vic. They would talk animatedly across me, almost oblivious to my presence, making it hard to avoid the smell of tea on their breath and the odd drop of saliva that flew in my direction. They would share jokes and moan in unison about the abilities of certain players. I still believe the simultaneous groan of exasperation that reverberates around Upton Park when one of their boys puts a pass astray is unsurpassed by any other ground. I wanted all that. To be sat with people I knew, my friends, sharing the experience.

The first time I saw Tottenham Hotspur in the flesh was from that seat at Upton Park in 1991. I was drawn to Gary Lineker, who I'd seen playing for England in the World Cup in Italy a year before. He scored Tottenham's only goal in a 2-1 defeat, a result that did nothing to dampen my new-found love. Even in defeat they had played some great football, something my eight-year-old eyes had begun to open up to. My mind was made up. My friends at the time were all Spurs fans, and I was eager to see them at school on Monday morning to talk about the match.

I realise now that it was the possibility of going along to the football with my friends that made supporting Spurs all the more appealing. I envisioned myself and my mates, twenty or thirty years into the future, sat at the Lane and slating the latest crop of useless clowns that dared to pull on the lilywhite shirt, harking back to the glory days. We would be just like Grandad and Vic.

The football world had changed though. Prices were going up and up. Groups who used to stand together on the terraces were separated by regulated and restricted seating. There was no way I'd get to go to matches regularly enough to develop the camaraderie in the stands that my grandad had. I soon lost touch with my Spurs-supporting friends from primary school and my trips to the Lane were sporadic at best. I ended up going with my mum, despite her own Hammers allegiance. I would badger her to take me, and like all mothers she wanted me to be safe, so she became my football companion for a while. I was now back in the same situation as before, only this time my mum had taken my grandad's place, stopping me from venting my emotions from the stands. I appreciate her actions now, but as a moody and self conscious teenager attending the football with my mother ranked alongside having a crap haircut or bad trainers in the social stakes.

I'd long since given up on going to the football regularly with mates. The choice of top-flight football teams on offer to kids from Essex is pretty broad: Tottenham, West Ham, Arsenal and Chelsea were the local options, as well as Manchester United for the glory hunters and Liverpool for the outdated glory hunters. There was no common ground among the groups of friends where I came from. There were few opportunities to go to Spurs with friends, where I could shout and swear unencumbered by the presence of an elder family member.

By the late nineties I had achieved a football emancipation of sorts. I could go on my own if I really wanted, but that was never an option for me. Football is a group activity. I was content in following the ups and downs of my beloved club from a distance, and having persuaded my mum to get Sky TV, more televised games were available to me than ever before. I became another one of the sofa supporters.

Twenty-one years on from that first encounter at Upton Park, after committing myself to Spurs, I still feel like I'm missing something.

*

The Premier League has now come of age. Over eighteen seasons, England's top flight has transformed into one of the world's leading leagues. It is beamed across the globe and has a television audience of over half a billion people in over 200 countries. The action is fast-paced, goals are spectacular and plentiful, and with Sky Sports providing the coverage, every conceivable angle is covered.

As football fans we live in a golden age. We are treated to 24-hour football news, bringing us up-to-the-minute stories from inside every club. There is televised football on offer almost every day of the week. As the Premier League has grown, the exposure and hyperbole that accompanies it has grown too. I'll be the first to admit that I'm guilty of buying into it all. I've been known to sit for hours, days even, as Sky Sports News looped over and over, waiting to hear even the faintest whisper of news about who Spurs might sign. I have watched the goals on *Match of the Day* then watched them again on *Goals on Sunday*. If I missed anything, I would find all the footage I need, usually with Arabic or Chinese commentary, on the internet.

That is unless Spurs lost, of course. If that happened, I would shut the football world out. It would cease to exist until the following Saturday when the chance to rectify a week's worth of humiliation would come swiftly to my aid. I would be unbearable to be around for days after a defeat. Where women can cite their monthly cycle as a reason for mood swings and irrational behaviour, my irritable and volatile temper could be blamed on a weekly cycle of hope, annoyance and despair. The worst part of it was its utter unpredictability because Spurs were utterly unpredictable. In the time that I have supported them, they have generally been very average. But 'average' hides the highs and lows – a Spurs supporter is exposed to moments of pure magic and inexorable joy suddenly followed by cataclysmic disaster, misery and dejection.

As a grown man I should keep a lid on my emotions, especially in the trivial world of football. However, I am not entirely at fault. There are some mitigating circumstances. Football matches are now given a life-or-death billing and the Darwinian significance of every game is contagious. In the current economic climate, it is very much a matter of survival. The amount of money at stake in football gives losing an almost terminal prognosis. This situation has resulted in the game's 'have-nots' performing a balancing act between their need for survival and their desire to succeed, leaving the 'haves' in a luxurious position of dominance.

It is the result of the omnipresent nature of the Premier League. Behind the façade of glitz and glamour is a sport that seems to have lost its way. It's easy for outsiders to say it's just a game, but when you invest financially, spiritually and emotionally in the fortunes of a football club, what is at stake becomes very real. Just ask the supporters at Portsmouth, Crystal Palace, Southend United or any number of other clubs that have been, or still are, a stroke of a pen away from oblivion. Football is not as fun as it used to be.

It got serious a while ago when Roman Abramovich upped the stakes at Chelsea. Now more clubs are controlled by super-rich businessmen. Manchester City's new oil-rich owners have allowed the club to pay £200,000 per week to a player deemed to be expendable by Spanish giants Barcelona. It is lunacy. The financial gulf between the fan in the stands and the millionaire on the pitch is vast. In fairness, players have short careers and are vulnerable to injuries that could snatch their livelihoods away from them at any time. A player has fifteen years to earn as much money as he can, but this money-driven mentality seems to eclipse the other reasons to play professional football. As players move from club to club seeking ever-higher wages, the connection between fans and the players they support is marginalised. It's hard to care about a guy who could well be trying to score against you in a few months time. The days of drinking with the players in the bar after the game have long since departed, and the celebrity lifestyle, fast cars and beautiful women detract from what it is that players are supposed to be doing: playing for their club and in turn playing for the fans. They kiss the badge and run to the crowd every time they score, but these partisan displays are all part of the show.

How important are you to your club? The chances are that the answer is 'not very' if your club resides in the Premier League for any significant length of time. Premier League clubs, whether they intend to or not, take full advantage of their fans' devotion. In the world of big business, no other companies can boast the brand loyalty that a football club possesses. This is why clubs can get away with ticket price hikes year after year and why they release three marginally-different redesigned shirts every season. The serfs in the stands are mere turnstile statistics. Premier League crowds have topped 200 million people since its inaugural year, during which time the average ticket price has risen from around £11.50 to £44. We no longer get treated like fans but like ordinary punters, a bum on a seat. We buy the shirts, the scarves, the mugs, the celebratory DVDs; all because we want to feel a part of our club, like we are making a difference, but our relevance is only reflected in the balance sheets and not the trophy cabinet.

As much as I love my club, I can't truly say I am connected to it as supporters were 25 or 30 years ago. I've never sat in the same seat twice at White Hart Lane. I was on the season ticket waiting list for years and paid my annual dues as a club member, but what I got in return dwindled while the price crept up. You can't see a game at White Hart Lane now for less than £30, and while that is excusable on the odd occasion, it is impossible to sustain. Even if I had a season ticket, I would be surrounded by strangers. For me, an experience like that would be as empty as watching a match alone in a busy pub. Football is a social event and should be shared with friends and family. My friends are a collection of Arsenal, Chelsea, Liverpool and West Ham fans. Those that say they support Spurs do so only in a vaguely interested manner and would have no real desire to accompany me week-in week-out to see them, especially when it costs around £800 a year to do so.

To say I'm disillusioned with my football club would be wrong. I love Spurs, but the reality is that they are part of a bigger problem endemic in top-flight English football. The romance has gone and has been replaced by season after season of predictable outcomes. Sky dress up every game as match of the season, and for a whole week players are trotted out to tell their fans how much they are up for it and how much the game means to them. We get served up Grand Slam Sundays, Survival Saturdays and derbies galore. Inevitably, they rarely live up to the hype. Formations have become more conservative. Lone strikers are now commonplace and defences are screened by two combative midfielders. It's all too clinical, and with what's at stake now, it's entirely understandable.

The only variable that exists in football these days is the size of a club's bank balance. Success begets success, failure is becoming irreversible, and there appears to be no end to this cycle. The best players flock to the richest clubs because they can afford the highest salaries. This isn't wrong as such, it is basic economics after all, but it does maintain a status quo that has caused the game to stagnate. A player as gifted as Matt Le Tissier, for example, would not stay at a club like Southampton for his whole career in this day and age. Players with his ability previously allowed smaller clubs to compete on a more level playing field. Now any teenage talent is spotted and snapped up by bigger clubs further up the financial food chain, often before they have made their full debut.

In the twenty years since I saw that first game at Upton Park, only fourteen teams have lifted a major piece of domestic silverware. That is sixty trophies – twenty First Division or Premier League titles, twenty FA Cups and twenty League Cups – claimed by less than 15% of the teams in English professional football. In the twenty years that preceded my introduction to football, 23 teams or 25% of football league clubs were successful in those same three prizes. The decades immediately after the war give a similar 25% outcome (and this despite the League Cup only coming into existence in 1961). The chance of glory is the life blood of all football fans. When that chance becomes as slim as it has done for most clubs, and players start to care more about who pays them rather than who plays them, fan interest will fade. I'm not saying the be-all and end-all of football supporting is counting the silverware your club accumulates, but there needs to be a thin seam of hope. Something to dream about.

There has to be an alternative to the corporate cash cow of the Premier League, some way of uniting friends every other week to follow a common cause. A place where every pound spent on pies, pints and programmes is appreciated and doesn't go to waste. Where the men out on the park don't earn more than their egos can take, and where the supporters can literally reach out and touch their heroes.

*

In February 2010, I was accompanied by my girlfriend, Stacey, and ten friends to watch Leyton Orient take on the fallen giants of Leeds United. It was a birthday outing, and like I usually did before most birthdays, I'd scanned the fixture lists across London and Essex for a suitable game to attend. The Orient-Leeds fixture jumped out at me. Leeds were one of the casualties of the Premier League. Having splashed big money to live the dream during the nineties, even reaching the Champions League semi-final in 2001, they overspent and the house of cards tumbled down. Now they were pushing for automatic promotion from League One and were likely to bring a strong team from Yorkshire. Despite the cold weather and poor quality of football that ensued because of boggy conditions, everyone had a great day – helped by the surprise result, a 1-1 draw in which Leeds only scraped an equaliser in injury time. It led to a chorus of 'we should do this more often' and as we headed towards the shelter and warmth of a pub off Bishopsgate, a giddy sense of excitement grew in me as a plan formed in my mind.

The vague idea had been floating round my head for a while. I pitched it over a couple of beers to general approval and the nodding of heads. Then it snowballed and gathered all sorts of additions and glorious twists until everyone in the vicinity, including people I'd just met, became advocates to the plan. Inevitably, those that voiced their immediate interest sobered up and slowly but surely stepped away from it, clinging to whatever excuse suited them: time, money, other commitments.

It was hardly a groundbreaking idea. It was neither difficult, daring nor out of the ordinary: buying a season ticket at Leyton Orient Football Club. I had been to watch Orient a handful of times over the years. I used to head up from Essex with a mate of mine when I was about sixteen. We would play a few frames of snooker at Leyton Billiard Hall, try and get served in a local pub and then wander over to the ground for the game. I'd seen a League Cup tie against Newcastle United and play-off matches in the old Second Division against Hull City. The atmosphere was always lively and passionate but never hostile. The ground is old-fashioned, tucked away behind rows of terraced houses just off the main high street. I could imagine the local residents stepping out from their front doors on match days, draped in scarves and rosettes, walking straight across the road and through the turnstiles. This was a club at the heart of a community and with plenty of heritage and history behind it despite a lack of tangible success. I had an affection for the club and continued to pay the occasional visit to watch the O's for a football fix every other season or so. They became a second team of sorts and I would keep an eye out for their scores as Saturday's results rolled in.

A season ticket at Orient ticked all my boxes. As a resident of Spitalfields in east London, the short trip down the Central Line made the journey time to and from games a cinch. My day job sat conveniently on the Central Line too, at Chancery Lane, should I need to nip to Brisbane Road for a midweek evening game after work.

It was bound to be affordable and better value for money than a Premier League club. Over the last decade, season ticket and matchday prices at Premier League grounds have been the subject of much debate. The average season ticket price for the capital's elite clubs was upwards of £600. At £300 for 23 home matches, Orient presented itself as a very reasonable alternative.

The standard of football was going to be pretty decent. While League One football may not be as aesthetically appealing as top-flight football, there is at least a relatively level playing field, making each season an unpredictable one. The casualties of Premier League survival battles, relegation-induced player exoduses and a failure to adapt quickly to change has created a graveyard of well-known clubs in the lower reaches of the Football League: Leeds United (who did win promotion despite their draw at Orient), Manchester City, Nottingham Forest and Charlton Athletic have all spent recent seasons scrapping away in the third tier of English football.

Most importantly, for the first time in my life I would be able to regularly watch the sport I love with a group of friends. We would enjoy pre-match beers, half-time pies and the post-match dash to the local to celebrate or commiserate the afternoon's result. The majority of the games would be played at the traditional kick-off time of 3 o'clock on Saturday afternoon. Like so many of the customs in the English game, Premier League television coverage has ripped up the rule book on kick-off times. Games switch and change to suit the programming schedules. 3 o'clock on Saturday afternoon would now be sacrosanct to us. Our lives would be planned around it, our weekdays would be nothing more than a climactic build-up to the main event on a Saturday afternoon.

Out of the group of twelve who attended the Leeds game that wintery afternoon in February, four of us made the pledge. It was an opportunity for us all. Jamie, who had always enjoyed football but never had a team to call his own, was an entirely blank canvas. He was completely open to the club, like a man on a first date with the potential girl of his dreams. Murph and Chas, two lifelong Arsenal fans, were in the same situation as me. They too suffered from the enormity of the prices at their club. Now they had a chance to watch regular football with mates without club allegiances getting in the way.

Chas, who invariably makes a drama out of most ordinary things, took a little convincing, but the cheques were on their way to Brisbane Road during the closing games of the 2009-10 season. Chelsea clinched a league and cup double, taking the title by one point from Manchester United and beating a long-since relegated Portsmouth in the FA Cup final. More importantly, my beloved Tottenham Hotspur finished fourth, meaning that not only had they broken up Sky TV's gratingly monikered 'Big Four' of United, Chelsea, Arsenal and Liverpool, they had also booked their place in Europe's foremost club competition for the first time since the 1960s. Perhaps I was leaving the Premier League just as it was turning a corner and the predictable run of results was coming to an end?

'This had better be bloody worth it,' I said to Murph one afternoon by email. 'First time in twenty years of supporting Spurs that they do well and I commit to League One football.'

'Of course it will,' he replied a few minutes later. 'Anyway, too late now, I've sent the applications off.'

The next nine months of our lives were set. 23 games lay ahead, maybe more if Orient did well in a cup run – although after a season in which Orient had just escaped relegation by the skin of their teeth and got knocked out of the FA Cup in the first round, we knew bright moments such as cup runs were few and far between in Leyton. As a Spurs fan, I was used to the genuine hope of silverware and expected a top-half finish as a bare minimum. I would have to get used to reduced expectations, where relegation was a very real prospect, silverware was what you ate your dinner with and general club survival is far from guaranteed.

It cost me £300 to experience this way of life. It was a situation many at Brisbane Road were born and raised with, but one in which Murph, Chas, Jamie and I were entering of our own volition. I was sacrificing the potential opportunity to see AC Milan, Barcelona and Bayern Munich, giants of the European game, to watch AFC Bournemouth, Walsall and MK Dons. Would it be worth it? I had no idea. This could be a very long nine months.

August 2010

I work in the heart of London's legal district for one of the world's leading legal publishers, a role I somehow fell into after a year travelling. Needing a full-time job after twelve months of bumming around, drinking, partying and working up a large debt, the position had a decent salary for a 23-year-old with no proper work experience aside from pulling pints in busy night spots. A law and politics degree helped me get my foot in the door for an interview and then my big gob took over. For some reason I spent practically every minute of the 45 that I was allotted talking about football. Playing football, writing about football, watching football – I worked in all sorts of contrived football examples to help cover my lack of real achievements. When asked why I wanted the job, the best reason my brain could conjure on the spot was, 'well, I'm not getting any younger'.

Somehow I got the job in spite of my seemingly inadequate responses and had been stuck there for almost four years with the same unchanging role, minimal pay rises and a sore head from banging it on a glass ceiling. Fortunately the job was easy, stress free and had given me ample time and freedom to indulge in what I enjoy most: following football.

Orient were due to play their first game of the season away at Yeovil Town on 7th August. Away matches weren't something we had discussed in the build up to the season and certainly weren't something Stacey had considered. It's unfortunate that Stace, someone who has no interest in or appreciation of football, has ended up with someone as besotted with the game as I am. She has even gone as far as suggesting that my single-minded passion has made her dislike the sport even more. In the first eighteen months of our relationship I tried to get her into it on every possible occasion, but any good that I did promoting the positives of the game was usually undone by my bad mood if Spurs lost. Then we'd be back at square one, or if it was possible, even further back than square one.

Now we sit at an impasse. I have given up trying to convert her and realise she will never become a football fan, and she treats my love of football in the same way she treats all of my other foibles: grudging acceptance.

With the first game of the season on the near horizon, it struck me that I knew precisely nothing of the Orient first team. Not wanting to come across as a complete novice were I to speak with anyone outside of our intrepid quartet, I felt the right and proper thing to do was to devote some time in my unexciting and uninspiring work schedule to immersing myself in the club.

A stroke of good fortune was that Orient had signed an almost entirely new team for the coming season. As an outsider venturing into a realm that was not my own, it was comforting to think that even some die-hard fans who had followed the O's for decades probably knew as little about their first team as I did.

Thankfully, it no longer takes a monumental amount of research to become familiar with a new football team, on a basic level in any case. I wasn't after forensic detail, just names and player histories. A browse around Wikipedia, the internet oracle of knowledge, was all that was required.

Although swotting up was necessary in the short term, it did seem a little like the scene from the nineties hooligan flick *I.D.* when undercover coppers, looking to infiltrate the local firm of fictitious Shadwell Town, have to commit all kinds of incidents from the club's history to memory in just a few days by way of authenticating their new personas. Unlike *I.D.* there was little chance of savage and violent repercussions if I forgot some esoteric event from the club's past, so with the pressure off I settled to browsing, note-taking and memorising:

- Russell Slade, manager, journeyman with his eighth club, took over at end of last season

- Steven Dawson, midfielder, young Irishman, acquired from Bury, new club captain
- Dean Cox, winger, played for Slade at Brighton
- Elliot Omozusi, right-back, former Fulham player
- Terrell Forbes, centre-back, also played under Slade but at Yeovil

Once I'd finished making notes I tore the pages from my notepad, folded them and slipped them inside my jacket pocket. I read through the scribbled observations for the next couple of days as I walked the 45-minute slog from my house to place of work on Chancery Lane. By the end of the week I felt fully versed in who played where, what their previous season had been like and who was likely to start the game against Yeovil.

With the distraction of learning about my new team, I almost forgot about the goings on at my old one. The draw for the qualifying round of the Champions League was near and the message boards and blogs were alive with talk of who Spurs might get and whether they could progress to the group stages. Spurs were in a pot with various other non-automatic qualifiers and could face any number of tricky ties including Ajax, Sevilla, Sampdoria and Dynamo Kiev. It would be a complete anti-climax if Spurs fell at the first hurdle after the trials and tribulations they went through to break into the top four and reach the Champions League. Fans were well aware the same fate befell Everton the last time a team other than the 'Big Four' had finished in a Champions League qualifying spot in 2005.

The draw was made in Switzerland on the Friday before the Football League big kick-off. I sat at my desk on Chancery Lane with the computer surreptitiously switched to the UEFA website and headphones on, waiting eagerly for the draw to start.

A potentially tricky tie against east European opposition was probably the worst case scenario, while the Swiss league runners-up, Young Boys Bern, were the weakest team in the draw. I had my fingers, toes and eyes crossed for that particular ball to be plucked from the pot alongside Spurs.

Once the UEFA officials finished blabbing on about the convoluted draw format, we were underway. First to be drawn was my preferred choice, Young Boys. I held my breath, prayed to however many deities I could remember from my RE lessons at school and hoped fate would be kind. I heard the balls clatter together as they tumbled and mixed in the pot. A pause. A twist and a click as the little capsule opened. An unfurling of paper. A pronouncement:

'Tott-in-ham Hot-spor.'

I punched the air. The best draw possible had been hand-delivered by a faceless suit a couple of hundred miles away. Emails and text messages flooded in almost immediately, the majority of which said things like 'easy', 'get in' or 'you lucky bastards!'

A couple of messages did take the gloss off my good mood, however. One, from a Spurs-supporting friend, said, 'great draw! Are we going to the game?' It reminded me that having discarded my club membership in favour of Orient, and with the tickets likely to be harder to come by than an audience with the Pope, I had as much chance of Harry Redknapp naming me among the substitutes as I did of getting a seat in the stands. Champions League football was going to be an armchair-only experience for me.

A second message, this one from Chas, was even more unnerving. 'Can still see you losing,' was his simple edict. Although this was just a typical piece of anti-Spurs sniping from my Arsenal-supporting pal, he reminded me of Tottenham's major flaw: the ability to make the incredibly easy look incredibly difficult. In a little over ten days, we would see.

In true English footballing tradition, the dawn of the new season was greeted with a blanket of grey cloud. Halfway through breakfast the phone rang. Murph's excitable voice greeted me and launched straight into his thoughts for the day's game.

'Looking at the team we've got, I'm thinking play-offs maybe, but then we nearly got relegated last season so I might be being a bit overconfident. Slade's supposed to be a real motivator though, and by all accounts Dawson could've played Championship level but chose to sign for us. What do you reckon?'

During Murph's enthusiastic monologue I couldn't help but notice his use of 'we' as pronoun. Still yet to set foot inside Brisbane Road for an Orient game this season, and having only ever been a passive observer at a handful of games in the past, I wasn't sure whether a £300 invest-ment constituted enough of a bond for the word 'we' to be appropriate just yet. These connections take time.

I managed to force out a few hopeful opinions for the season ahead through a mouthful of egg and toast, but after a five-minute conversation we arrived squarely at the conclusion that we had absolutely no idea what was going to happen. We were more than happy about that.

Every season in the Premier League, the same five or six teams will finish at the top and the champions will more often than not come from one of three teams: Manchester United, Chelsea or Arsenal. This is how it has been for at least a decade. The only real unpredictability comes at the other end of the table, but invariably the three teams who were promoted from the Championship the previous season are among those struggling to avoid the drop ten months later.

In stark contrast, the division in which we were about to immerse ourselves was wide open. League One is refreshed by seven new sides every season, three relegated from the Championship and four promoted from League Two. It already contained some pretty big names such as Brighton and Hove Albion, Southampton, Huddersfield Town and Charlton; this season they were joined by Shef-field Wednesday and Peterborough United. With trips as far north as Carlisle and Hartlepool and as far south as Plymouth and Exeter to contend with, players would put in plenty of miles on the team bus. The margins between all 24 clubs were so tight that one 25-goals-a-season striker or a single dependable defender in the squad might make or break the season. Whoever went up would need steely determination and luck on their side.

Where Orient sat in all of this was the greatest mystery of all, and the solution was unlikely to be revealed after one single Saturday afternoon. Murph was spending the day at a family barbeque and I planned to spend the day in front of the TV watching the scores come in, so I promised to keep him updated.

Stacey's work at a commercial art gallery in Westbourne Grove near Notting Hill meant that, more often than not, she would be working on Saturday afternoon. However, this opening Saturday of the season she had taken a rare day off due to sickness and was tucked up in bed. I was playing nurse in one room while trying to keep up to date with the scores in the other.

Sky's *Soccer Saturday* is a staple for any football supporter unable to make it to a live game. The format is simple: one host (the venerable Jeff Stelling) and a panel of ex-professionals watch the 3 o'clock games on unseen monitors and furnish the enthralled viewer with minute-by-minute updates throughout the afternoon. As a Spurs fan, I'm used to seeing the score I'm most interested in constantly ticking over at the bottom of the screen and a live update from the pundit every ten minutes or so. Things would be a little different today. With the Premier League season still a week away from kick-off, the panel were casting their eyes over some select Championship matches. I was expecting at least an outside reporter doing his bit to camera for the Orient match. Unfortunately, the silence from Yeovil's Huish Park was deafening. I remained completely in the dark.

Then, with 12 minutes on the clock, the vidiprinter flashed up a goal. Yeovil had scored. I texted Murph with a simple message: 'bollocks, a goal down'.

Silence descended once more. For the next half an hour, Yeovil Town and Leyton Orient football clubs may as well have not existed. Relief came just before half-time, when a second goal from the West Country flashed up on the vidiprinter. Alex Revell, Orient's summer signing from Southend United, had bagged an equaliser. Exalting in triumph and waking Stace from her sickbed slumber, I had barely sent off the jubilant news of 'gooooooalll!!! 1-1' to Murph before a new scoreline appeared at the foot of the screen: Yeovil 2 Leyton Orient 1. Cursing loudly and firing off another text to break the bad news, I slumped back on the sofa.

The televisual silence continued in the second half. I hoped that this wasn't the usual experience for lower league teams. Receiving updates on a game you can't see is critical in supplying the one thing football supporters survive on: hope. Not knowing anything was a kind of torture; as the Stereophonics once said, 'it's the not knowing that kills you'. I began to wonder whether I'd missed an update, or maybe the line had been lost from Yeovil. I even got last-minute butterflies in my stomach as I hoped for a last gasp equaliser, but it was in vain.

Full-time whistles began to go across the country and the long-awaited update from Yeovil came through as a confirmed result. The O's had lost their opening game of the season. 'Game over,' I texted, 'it's going to be a long season!'

Murph's philosophical response of, 'oh well, it's what we're in it for,' was a far cry from his positive phone call I'd received a few hours before, but it was true in its sentiment. Besides, with only one match out of a mammoth 46-game season gone, losing wasn't the worst thing in the world. A win on our first outing to Brisbane Road would more than make up for it.

I noticed during the advert breaks throughout the afternoon that there was a small change in the media representation of the Premier League in its promotional material. Every player montage would have to contain a member of the Big Four in some kind of inclusive symmetry and a virtual nod to the teams that Sky seem to really care about. Rooney would score, Gerrard would run by, Lampard would shoot and Fabragas would slide on his knees. Surprisingly though, an addition had been made to their cast of Big Four stars. The logical option would have been a Spurs player to be represented in there, recognition of their having done the impossible and broken into the top four. But no, it was Manchester City's Carlos Tevez who joined the party. A ball hadn't even been kicked in the Premier League and the petrodollars of Abu Dhabi had thrust City into Sky's elite selection of favourite clubs. It shouldn't bother me, and it may sound like sour grapes over a trivial point, but if suspicious minds such as my own look for evidence of a Sky agenda, it's things like this that give them away.

My contempt for Sky favouritism continued into the next week during the build up to the Community Shield. Traditionally the shield, competed for by the Premier League and FA Cup winners of the previous season, is the start of season opener. Manchester United and Chelsea were the uninspiring match-up this year, as they had been for three of the past four seasons. Most pundits predicted that the result would be an indication of who would win the Premier League. A sad indictment really, considering there were eighteen other teams and the season was yet to get under way.

From the first whistle, the effort put in by both sides was negligible. Commentators tried to talk it up, but the game was flat. Even the Wembley crowd seemed subdued. Row upon row of replica shirt-wearing families sat quietly waiting for something to happen. If this was the curtain-raiser, who would want to stay and watch the rest of the show? As it was, United ran out 3-1 winners, with Chelsea only coming to life with 15 minutes left.

Perhaps I was being nostalgic, but I was sure the Community Shield (or the Charity Shield as it used to be known) used to be more dynamic and hold a lot more interest for the neutral. I recalled one such shield match from a few years before. On a day trip to some old stately home my mum wanted to visit, my excitement and interest in the game was so great that I insisted I stay in the car in the car park to listen to the game on the radio as Manchester United beat Newcastle 4-0, leaving my Mum to trudge off on her own to look round the grounds. With the way the shield is treated now, as a glorified friendly, perhaps it would be better to have an All-Stars or North v South game instead. At least then the pretence of competition is taken away and the fun can return.

After scoring, albeit unsuspectingly with his face, young Mexican Javier Hernandez was being praised from all quarters, typical of the modern trend where a young player who shows any sign of promise has all sorts of pressure and hype heaped on him without him being allowed to develop naturally. Instead of telling us who's the best and who isn't, I'd quite like it if the media let us make our own minds up for a change.

<u>Friday 13th August 2010</u>
<u>Orient v Charlton Athletic</u>

Having followed up the Yeovil loss with victory at Swindon in the League Cup during the week, the cloud of defeat had been replaced by optimism in time for Orient's first home game. An exciting League Cup second round draw at home against Premier League West Bromwich Albion meant an early-season upset could be in order, and a good result against promotion-fancied Charlton would help the team get in the giant-killing mood.

I was looking forward to regular Saturday afternoon 3 o'clock kick-offs without the threat of the Sky Sports listings spoiling the schedule. Life rarely goes to plan, however. The opening home game against Charlton was chosen by Sky to be televised live, at 7:45 on a Friday evening.

I was still as excited about going to a match as I could remember. Although three points would be good, winning or losing didn't really come into it. Having no emotional connection to the club, results were less important than the experience. As I left the office that Friday evening, I couldn't help but feel that this was the start of an exciting new journey.

I arrived at Leyton tube station a little after 6pm, just 25 minutes after leaving my desk in central London, and looked out across the road and down past the A12 to the skeletal frames and structures of the emerging Olympic Park. Murph arrived minutes later, smiling widely and pumping his fists in the air. After a few pints in the King Harold pub on High Road, we met still-suited Jamie and headed back up the road towards the stadium, joining a stream of Orient and Charlton fans snaking their way to Brisbane Road.

Brisbane Road is not actually the name of Leyton Orient's home ground, nor has it ever officially been so. It was formally known as Osbourne Road for many years, but has since been rechristened the Matchroom Stadium after club chairman Barry Hearn's sport promotion business. Normally clubs that rename their stadium do so to generate extra revenue by selling the naming rights to external sponsors, like Coventry City's Ricoh Arena or Arsenal's

Emirates Stadium. I've never heard anyone refer to the Matchroom Stadium with its official title, and the club can't generate any extra revenue as the ground is named after the owner's company. It's an odd situation and one that seems utterly pointless. As a traditionalist, I believe that football grounds should be known by a geographical landmark, street name or district like Anfield or White Hart Lane. Through habit and a stubborn streak I always stick to the old names, so to me Brisbane Road it is.

Whatever name it goes under, Brisbane Road is an unusual ground. Its 9,271-capacity stands are punctuated on each corner by a four-storey apartment block. These blocks not only serve as a clever way of making extra revenue for the club but are also an ideal vantage point for residents who want to take advantage of some free football. It must be an interesting place to live, although you'd need the patience of a saint to put up with chants of 'we can see you washing up!' reverberating around your kitchen every couple of weeks as fans peer through your windows.

We wanted to make sure we were positioned at the heart of the Orient support. From our trip to the Leeds United game in February, we knew that the best place would be behind the goal at the Buckingham Road end. Known as the Tommy Johnston Stand in honour of Orient's all-time leading goal scorer who passed away in September 2008, the stand has a single bank of seats stretching back around twelve rows and holds just over 1300 fans. This would be a perfect place to assimilate ourselves into O's fan culture, and who knows, maybe start a few chants of our own.

Still waiting for Chas, who had all our season tickets, we perched ourselves on a street corner. At 7:15pm his lumbering figure came out of the park on Buckingham Road. Without saying a word he unzipped his jacket, proudly revealing a new, gleaming-white Orient away shirt.

It was time to see the seat I would call home for the next nine months: Row J, Seat 81. It was in a perfect spot, giving an unobstructed view from behind the goal and positioned in the heart of the Orient support, which had upped a few decibels in anticipation of kick-off. Looking out at the vista, I was pleasantly surprised to see a healthy-looking attendance. The novelty of the first game of the season coupled with a London derby seemed to have attracted plenty of punters, although a fair number of them were sat to our right in the away section.

A bite of my pie at just the wrong moment, as the players came out of the tunnel, left me unable to clap or cheer my first sighting of the team. Choking on molten steak and kidney, the juices dribbling down my chin, the superstitious side of me wondered whether it was an ominous sign. The atmosphere was fantastic, with plenty of loud chants of 'Orient, Orient' accompanied by a percussive thump on the corrugated wall at the back of the stand. Derby matches always tend to encourage supporters to crank up the volume and it seemed lower league ones were no different.

Once the match got underway, I noticed a guy sat directly in front of me. He was peering intently into his lap where his iPhone was showing the live Sky coverage of the game. At least he'll have got a decent replay of the first goal, which silenced the crowd after half an hour. Seemingly out of nothing, Charlton snatched the lead after a looping header from a hopeful cross beat Orient's goalkeeper Jamie Jones. It certainly soured the half-time pint for the Brisbane Road faithful, but as mere Orient novices we glugged ours down, still enjoying the experience.

The crowd noise returned as the second half kicked off and almost raised the roof from the stand on 50 minutes. Orient's veteran forward Scott McGleish picked up a ball from diminutive winger Dean Cox just inside the area and drilled it low into the net, sending the home fans into raptures. I looked down the row to see Jamie punching the air and Murph leaping onto Chas' back in delight. It wasn't taking them long to get into the spirit. 'He's here, he's there, he's every-fucking-where, Scott McGleish, Scott McGleish,' the crowd chorused, and we joined them. The beauty of football chants. They take two seconds to learn and a lifetime to forget.

The positive mood of the home fans was improved even further when Charlton's Christian Dailly saw red for a second bookable offence, but that was to prove the high point. Orient turned up the pressure on ten-man Charlton but slowly ran out of ideas. Two breakaway Charlton goals, the last of which came in the 94th minute, stopped any chance of a winning start to our season as Orient fans.

'At least Charlton are supposed to be title contenders,' Murph said bitterly as we left the stadium and headed for the tube.

'One lucky header and two goals on the break was all they got,' I said. 'That was never a 3-1 game!'

We were genuinely pissed off. After all the build up and waiting to get going, we'd had a sudden realisation that we were following a club that isn't too familiar with success. Two league games, two defeats, no points.

It didn't get much better watching Spurs a few days later either. What I thought would be a comfortable ride into the group stages of the Champions League turned into a nightmare within half an hour as Young Boys, at home on their plastic pitch, went 3-0 up. I refused to look at the mocking messages appearing on my phone as the goals rained in. A comeback of sorts made it 3-2 on the night but didn't improve my mood.

The following weekend, I almost entirely avoided football. Stace and I went to Hylands Park in Chelmsford for the V Festival. The football-free zone was partly enforced by poor mobile reception, but I had an inkling that Stacey considered the weekend to be 'our time' and intrusion from football would be frowned upon. I did manage to sneak a quick phone call to Chas in the never-ending queue for beer. Orient had earned their first point of the season away at Southampton and Spurs had won away at Stoke. Maybe things weren't too bad after all.

Tuesday 24th August 2010
Orient v West Bromwich Albion

The second round of the League Cup seemed to come very soon after the first, so our second trip to Brisbane Road would be another evening game. The experience was a far cry from our first outing. Despite Premier League opposition, albeit of the lesser variety, the crowd was poor. Perhaps most people had better things to do than watch an inevitable beating for £20 on a Tuesday evening. The subdued atmosphere seemed to spill on to the pitch as a dull game ended 2-0 to the visitors. We weren't even paying all that much attention to the game, spending much of the second half listening to Chas harp on about a bird he was seeing. The most entertainment came before kick-off as the teams were warming up. A bloke standing idly behind the goal took his eye off the pitch at precisely the wrong time and was hit hard by a stray shot from a West Brom player. The striker promptly apologised to the shaken fan before doing exactly the same thing again a minute later.

We made arrangements for the Exeter game on Saturday on our way to catch the tube and went our separate ways back to Bethnal Green and South Woodford. I wandered down the steps at Leyton station, reading the evening's programme and onto the train that pulled in almost immediately. As the doors closed I heard a sniggering and looked up to see Chas and Murph grinning at me.

'Alright Ad?' Murph said, stifling a laugh.

I thought for a moment and looked around. It slowly dawned on me, as the train pulled out of the station, that while engrossed in the contents of my programme I'd jumped on a train on the wrong side of the platform.

'Oh bugger!' I moaned, shooting Chas and Murph a defeated look as they pissed themselves laughing in the corner of the carriage.

Having seen off Young Boys in a 4-0 stroll, banishing the jitters of the previous week, Spurs were through to the Champions League group stage. Their progress almost passed me by with the Orient match and a job interview on Thursday. Checking the BBC website as soon as I remembered, I saw that we couldn't have got a much harder group: reigning champions Inter Milan, Dutch champions FC Twente and German side Werder Bremen, who had seen off Sampdoria in the play-off round. It was probably a good thing to get a challenging group. Having almost gone out to weaker opposition, tougher group games should banish the complacency that often haunts Spurs. Tottenham playing at the San Siro would be a highlight to look forward to as well.

Saturday 28th August 2010
Orient v Exeter City

At last, a Saturday match at Brisbane Road, and the sun came out too. We arranged to meet at the ground as early as possible to pick up tickets for the Dagenham and Redbridge away match the following weekend – a nice gentle away trip along the District Line for a London derby seemed an ideal way to continue our assimilation into Orient life.

I stopped by Jamie's flat on my way to Bethnal Green station to pick up his season ticket, needed to purchase the ticket for the Daggers game, as he favoured turning up fashionably late for most occasions. True to form, he wasn't remotely ready to leave. He was stood in his room, thumping house music turned up loud enough to be heard in the street, dressed only in his boxer shorts, deliberating over what trainers to wear. Leaving him to it, I headed off to the ground where Murph and his fiancée Danielle were waiting for me at the ticket office on Oliver Road. Danielle was taking Chas' place for the day as the big man was off in Clapham getting his trance music fix at the SW4 music festival.

During the West Brom game, we discovered the Leyton Orient Supporters Club tucked away next to the club shop and ticket office on Oliver Road. The fan-run establishment had a relaxed and jovial vibe. Feeling more comfortable in Brisbane Road and less like frauds sneaking into a private party, we decided to venture back for our pre-match pints.

A grey-haired gentleman with a tidy moustache and glasses, remembering us from the previous fixture, ushered us over to a small table by the door and suggested we join the club. For just £11 we were able to enjoy the welcoming and comfortable surroundings of the bar for an entire season. Knowing that we were likely to spend many enjoyable beer-filled hours within its walls over the coming months, and that a portion of the joining fee and bar takings would go directly to the club itself (since being founded in 1978, the Supporters Club has donated almost £800,000 directly to the football club), the decision was a simple one.

Jamie arrived, having finally solved his footwear dilemma, which prompted us to finish our drinks and head to our seats. As kick-off approached we chatted with the group of lads behind us who, having been die-hard supporters their whole lives, were the root cause of much of the chanting that filled the Tommy Johnston Stand on match days.

The game was a joy. Having sat through two home defeats already and knowing that Orient occupied the foot of the table with just a single point, the transformation was spectacular. They were running Exeter ragged. Some of the passing moves were more worthy of Spurs' Champions League opposition than League One, and the three unanswered goals scored by Revell, McGleish and Cox were so confidently finished you'd have thought the team was flying high instead of languishing at the wrong end of the league table.

The full-time whistle brought a huge cheer and an ecstatic Russell Slade punched the air in delight. The fans cheerfully sang, 'he's got no hair but we don't care!' and in response the beaming manager reached for the brim of his baseball cap and doffed it in salutation, exposing his shiny, hairless pate. Supporters are easily pleased.

The Supporters Club was alive with chatter and laughter as we headed in for a celebratory pint. We texted Chas to tell him what he was missing as the goals flew in, but he could see the wider picture. The message on my phone at full-time read, 'great Orient result, we owned them!! Wigan haha!'

Wigan haha? With all the excitement of Orient's win, I'd forgotten Spurs were playing that afternoon too. On checking the results I saw a Hugo Rodellega goal ten minutes from time had clinched Wigan's first points of the season. Bloody typical. Up one minute, down the next, the danger of supporting two clubs it seemed. At least the Orient success would dampen my usual Spurs-induced misery for the next week.

If the beginning of August is the equivalent of English football settling gently into a hot spa, the end of the month is the moment someone turns on the bubbles. The final 24 hours are a whirlwind of frantic activity as the summer transfer window closes. Orient were never likely to be a part of these festivities, having done some astute and financially savvy business earlier in the summer. Spurs, however, never stray far from the headlines on deadline day.

The Sky Sports News team were as over-dramatic as ever, with snow-haired presenter Jim White almost imploding with excitement and hyperbole. Coverage periodically leapt to outside reporters stationed in every car park and training ground in the Premier League. As I got ready for work, I was laughing derisively at the seemingly endless fountain of speculation and guesswork that sprung forth from the TV. By lunchtime I had checked, double-checked and rechecked every website possible for news, abandoning curiosity and derision for sheer indulgence as my thirst for information spilled over into obsession. Ryan Babel was in a helicopter heading to White Hart Lane but Scott Parker had categorically turned us down. Story after story emerged, most of which I knew to be complete fantasy, but it was addictive viewing and I was hooked.

Hours went by with no confirmed news from White Hart Lane aside from the loan signing of a goalkeeper. Then at 5 o'clock, an hour before the deadline passed, a whisper reached my ears. Real Madrid's Dutch midfielder Rafael van der Vaart had reportedly agreed terms to switch to Spurs. I dashed home and immediately tuned back into Sky Sports News. The yellow breaking news ticker at the foot of the screen was devoid of updates. Had he signed? What was going on? A truly world class player may be winging his way to north London at that very moment. This was incredible news. Not since German legend Jürgen Klinsmann had signed for the club back in 1994 had I been this excited. The clock counted down, and as 6 o'clock struck on Big Ben to close the transfer window, nothing had been confirmed by the media.

Having started the day as a mildly amused onlooker, I ended it glued to the TV waiting for news. I thought a season at League One would remove me from the hype of the Premier League and make me immune to it, a kind of football vaccination. However, the disease was more potent than I thought, and I allowed myself to be swept back up in it. I tried to justify it to myself. I had all season to enjoy normality, but for one day I allowed myself to binge greedily on the bullshit and tittle-tattle of the Premier League. With any luck, I could wake up in September lucid and relaxed, ready to return to League One normality.

```
12.Rochdale...........P4 |W1 |D2 |L1 |F6 |A5 |5pts
13.Hartlepool United...P4 |W1 |D2 |L1 |F4 |A7 |5pts
14.Southampton.........P3 |W1 |D1 |L1 |F5 |A2 |4pts
15.Leyton Orient.......P4 |W1 |D1 |L2 |F6 |A6 |4pts
16.Yeovil Town.........P4 |W1 |D1 |L2 |F3 |A5 |4pts
17.Plymouth Argyle.....P4 |W1 |D1 |L2 |F3 |A6 |4pts
18.Notts County........P4 |W1 |D1 |L2 |F4 |A9 |4pts
```

September 2010

The news wasn't confirmed until 3:30 the next afternoon: Rafael van der Vaart had signed for Tottenham
Hotspur for around £8 million. After years of watching dross brought into the Spurs side in a last minute
panic while our best players jumped ship to bigger and
better clubs, we had signed some real quality at last. An
internationally-renowned midfielder, experienced Champions League player and World Cup finalist, complete
with continental swagger and glamorous wife, would now
be plying his trade at White Hart Lane. A 27-year-old
shouldn't be as excited as I was, but there is something
about a big-name signing that gets the juices flowing in
anticipation of some match-winning performances.

The thrill at van der Vaart's signing would never be felt in the same way at the O's. Who was there to get excited about at this end of the league ladder? At Orient, the drama of deadline day passed by like a distant thunderstorm. All the rumblings were on the horizon while it stayed quiet at Brisbane Road. Perhaps it was a good job there was no influx of new faces. Having only just dangled my feet in the shallow water of League One football, my knowledge of Orient players was far from encyclopaedic. I still barely knew the men I had chosen to follow.

As if recognising and remembering the different players was not a challenge enough, the times and dates of actual matches were passing me by too. The first round of the Johnstone's Paint Trophy was scheduled to take place on Wednesday evening. Open to the 48 teams in Leagues One and Two, the trophy allows lower-league clubs a reasonable chance of some silverware and the glamour of a Wembley final. Being almost oblivious to the existence of the competition, I was unaware Orient were playing until I looked at my phone on the bus on the way home from work. Orient, who started the season so poorly, had beaten promotion-chasing Brighton 2-0 at the Withdean Stadium with goals from Dean Cox and Ryan Jarvis. Enjoying a private and muted celebration in my seat, not wanting to panic fellow passengers into thinking I was a lunatic who usually made spontaneous outbursts in public, I sent a message to the boys with the good news and continued my merry way home, humming 'we've got

Tiny Cox, we've got Tiny Cox' to myself as I watched the city roll by.

Saturday 4th September
Dagenham and Redbridge v Orient

I awoke on the Saturday morning of our away day to Dagenham with a dry mouth and sore head, courtesy of a Friday night in the pub with Murph watching England hump a poor Bulgaria side 4-0. The result was made even more enjoyable by Spurs front-man Jermain Defoe bagging three of the goals. Knowing full well it was going to be another boozy day, with a mate's birthday gathering in Loughton following the Daggers match, I hopped in the shower to wash away the cobwebs and wolfed down a carb-heavy breakfast to fill my tender stomach for the day ahead.

My flat is situated a ten-minute walk from Aldgate East station on the District Line and it should have been an easy fourteen-stop journey to Dagenham East. That plan was dashed in typical London fashion when a quick glance at the weekend engineering works showed the District Line was closed along that exact stretch of track.

A couple of phone calls later and we had an alternative plan. I met Jamie on the way to Bethnal Green station, from where we headed to Murph's house in South Woodford. His bride-to-be, Danielle, had kindly offered to drive us the eight miles to the game. Piling into the back of their Volkswagen, grey clouds gathering overhead, we set off and picked our way through heavy traffic as rain began to fleck the windscreen.

It was still drizzling as we were dropped off in a housing estate on Rainham Road opposite the ground. We followed a small group of red-and-white shirted Orient fans down Victoria Road – after which Dagenham's stadium is traditionally named – and past the long steel-backed sides of the south stand. It is a cosy ground that holds a little over 6,000 fans. Orient had reportedly sold their entire allocation of tickets. As we entered the ground through the small brick turnstiles, we could see the away end had already begun to fill up with over an hour to go before kick-off.

Having only just shaken off the excesses of the night before, I made slow progress on my first pint. My recovering stomach gurgled loudly as alcohol re-entered it, but its protests were ignored. With plenty of time to kill, we stood leaning against a pillar, chatting idly in the open concreted refreshment area beneath the seats of the modern-looking Carling Stand, named after the lager rather than a former Dagenham legend.

With the hangover beginning to lift after munching through a huge sausage roll, the beer slid down a lot easier and the volume of our conversation began to creep up. By kick-off we were nicely oiled and had taken our place amongst the Orient faithful in the packed stand. The Dagenham fans filled the standing area at the opposite end and were crammed tightly in the stands along both sides of the pitch. The ground was full to capacity. The hosts were newly-promoted and this was the first league derby between the two clubs.

Our first away day, albeit just a handful of miles east of our usual surroundings, had us brimming with enthusiasm for the forthcoming match. It is often away fans who make the most noise. The novelty and unfamiliarity of the venue must have a psychological impact on a supporter, much in the same way that you never have as much fun at your own party as you do at someone else's. There is less expectation for a team playing away from home to win, making the burden of a result less of a concern. It is a care-free day out with several hundred souls who are there for the same reason. A win is just the icing on the cake.

Kick-off approached, and as the teams ran out onto the pitch, Murph broke into song. 'Orieeeeeeent, Orieeeeeeent, Orieeeeeeeent, Orieeeeeeent!' he bellowed, and the cry was taken up on all sides, by young and old. He turned round and grinned at us. 'I've never started a chant before,' he said, looking genuinely chuffed with himself.

'What about when we used to go down Billericay Town back in the day?' I suggested.

'Yeah, maybe, but there's a difference between getting 20 or 30 blokes to sing along and getting almost 2000 to do it. Tell you what though,' he added, 'I wouldn't have been able to do that at the Arsenal.' Raising his eyebrows he looked at Chas, who shrugged and nodded in agreement.

'No-one sings there half the time anyway,' Chas scoffed. 'It's a joke! Last time I went there, people were moaning about others standing and shushing them.'

'They pay almost £80 for a seat Chas,' I said, turning to face the pitch as the match kicked off, 'so I'm not surprised they don't want some big hairy lummox like yourself standing up ruining the view and spoiling the quiet ambience.'

The sun came out as the game got underway and was shining brightly in our eyes. Dagenham's tactics were clear: hoof the ball high and long down the pitch. With just eight minutes gone, the home side launched a deep cross into the Orient penalty area. Jamie Jones was stranded and the ball found Romain Vincelot's head, sending it crashing into the net. The home fans erupted with the first noise they'd made all afternoon. We slumped into our seats as torrents of abuse rained down at the Orient defence from all around us. Another poor start and another sloppy goal given away. When would they learn?

As Orient toiled in the middle of the park, Dagenham were happy to head out hopeful balls and lump them up to their big strikers. This was Sunday League park football at best and Orient had no answer to the route one tactics. The travelling crowd became increasingly fractious.

The second half started as badly as the first. Having barely taken our seats after downing our half-time refreshments, Dagenham won a corner down the far end.

'I hate set pieces,' Murph groaned, covering his mouth in nervous concern. 'We never look comfortable.'

No sooner had the words left his lips, the home fans were up and cheering as a second header from Vincelot flew past Jones and into the goal.

'I reckon that's it now,' Jamie said mournfully. 'Shall we just go and get pissed up? It's better than watching this tosh.'

'We've got all day to get boozed up,' I replied. 'Besides, it's only 2-0, and Dagenham are shit. They haven't won yet this season.'

I wish I'd listened to Jamie. The scoreline remained unchanged and the ever-increasing frustration of the Orient players destroyed whatever chance they had of a fight back. Even when Orient went close, Dagenham's goalkeeper, veteran Tony Roberts, pulled off some fantastic stops that defied his ample physique.

'I've scored against him you know,' I said casually as the rotund custodian sent a goal kick sailing over the halfway line.

'What? When?' Jamie asked, looking disbelievingly at me.

'Years ago,' I said. 'It was at a soccer school when I was ten and I got through to the shooting tournament final. He was the guest goalkeeper, played for QPR at the time. I strolled up and stroked it past him, cool as a cucumber.'

'Did you win?' Chas asked.

'Nah, he saved my other two efforts,' I said bitterly. 'Probably let the first one in to be honest. Gave me a mercy goal. Oh well. It's still better than those useless twats out there have done today.'

An old boy next to us who we recognised from the Supporters Club introduced himself. He began to tell us his Orient-supporting history. It turned out he had been following the O's for 64 years. Having been following the club for less than 64 days, we felt pretty humbled by his enthusiasm and loyalty. He'd seen it all, the good, the bad and the downright terrible, with little hope for glory. And there he was, 64 years later, still in the stands watching his team. Perhaps we weren't ready to criticise just yet. We hadn't earned the right.

As the game edged to full-time with little quality or adventure from either side, we entertained ourselves by shouting fat bloke gags at Roberts in goal. Taking it all in good fun, he rubbed his belly proudly before showing us what the score was on his gloved fingers. That shut us up pretty quickly.

We trudged out of the ground at full-time with the cheers of the home support ringing mockingly in our ears, making our way round the dirty brown houses and untidy front gardens at the back of the stadium towards the main road with its empty, boarded shops and tanning salons. It wasn't the most inspiring scene. The recent global economic turbulence seemed to have run through the town like a vacuum and sucked the life out of it. The football club, as in many deprived areas up and down the country, stood out among the rows of houses, its floodlights reaching into the sky. It offered a glimmer of brightness where all around it was cold, grey and in need of help.

We managed to jump into a cab outside an old run-down pub and speed off towards Loughton for our evening out. With the result, the league table, the grim surroundings and the beer wearing off, we were all gloomy. But it was nothing a good knees-up couldn't cure.

<u>Saturday 11th September 2010</u>
<u>Orient v Huddersfield Town</u>

The disappointment of the away day at Dagenham was soon forgotten. An eventful week passed by quickly: a hungover Sunday helping Stace with her art business on a stall at Spitalfields Market and an evening beneath the giant arc of Wembley Stadium watching Muse. The new stadium is an incredible venue. Having been to see both football matches and concerts there several times since its opening in 2007, I'm sure that it was worth the six-year wait.

The summer appeared to be dead and buried, but the following Saturday dawned dry and mild so I pulled on a pair of shorts. My waistline had begun to creep outwards after a summer of World Cup football and boozing in beer gardens, making my shorts somewhat tighter than they had been. I was going to have to watch myself on the pies and pints at Brisbane Road, or I would need to ask for my seat to be reinforced.

Home matches were coming thick and fast. Huddersfield Town were next up in E10. I walked over to Liverpool Street station with Stace just after lunch. She was heading to Ikea in Edmonton to buy picture frames while I went to Leyton to watch football and drink beer. I couldn't imagine a more polar-opposite afternoon.

'Go easy on the pies today beb,' she said, smiling and rubbing my stomach tenderly.

'Oi, less of that thank you,' I replied, sticking my bottom lip out and looking down on what was most definitely a slight paunch developing above my waist band. 'It's nothing a few runs can't solve.'

We kissed each other goodbye and went our separate ways. A group of Huddersfield fans got on the carriage with me. They seemed like decent, salt of the earth kind of fans, larking around, taking the piss out of each other. It made me wonder about the lengths some fans went to when they watch their team. Huddersfield was by no means a long way away, but it was hardly a short trip. Surely the expense outweighed the sporting gains? Our 'away day' to Dagenham was like a trip to the shop to buy a newspaper in comparison.

Meeting Murph at the station, we walked down High Road to the Supporters Club. My health drive starts now, I thought, as I approached the bar.

'Can I have a lime cordial please?' I asked cheerfully. It was clearly something rarely asked for on these premises, and I received a quizzical look before a huge quantity of lime cordial was tipped into a pint glass. Filling the vacant space with tap water, the barman handed over the drink and took my loose change. As I walked over to where Murph was standing, glued in front of the TV screen watching Everton take on Man United, I took a quick gulp. The sourness seemed to shrink my mouth, pulling it down at each corner, my eyes watered. Swallowing reluctantly, as though I was drinking poison, I turned around and headed back to the bar.

'You couldn't dilute this a bit more for me could you mate?' I asked. 'It's a tad strong.' Next time I'd just stick to the beer.

We stood watching the game on TV, waiting for Chas and Jamie to arrive. Jamie was flying back from a business trip to Dublin a day early just to get to the match, something most out of character for him since he usually took full advantage of a session on the company's expenses. As to Chas's whereabouts, we had no idea. Half an hour before kick-off, the big man arrived, lumbering in with a big smile on his face.

'Where've you been?' I asked.

'Just had a cracking night,' he began. 'I was round this bird's house. She's Jordanian,' he added after a pause.

'Jordanian?' Murph asked, looking amused and surprised.

'Well, half-Jordanian, half-Iranian,' Chas replied matter-of-factly.

As he began to tell us the mucky details of his sordid night rocking the casbah, Jamie arrived clutching a black leather holdall.

'How ya going, alright?' he said, shaking our hands one by one. 'Just got back from Dublin. Plane landed about two hours ago, haven't been home yet. How you doing for beers?'

A few months ago Jamie had no team and no interest at all in lower league football. Now he was cutting short business trips and dashing to games fresh from the runway. This was certainly a turn up for the books.

Jamie might have had an unexpected shift in behaviour, but it was the same old story for the O's. Huddersfield shot out of the blocks and were in front with a third minute goal after Orient dithered and failed to clear a free kick.

A couple of new faces in the O's line-up had us scratching our heads, but Paul, the guy who sat behind us in the Tommy Johnston Stand, soon filled us in on their biographies. His love and knowledge of all things Orient was borderline obsessive. Speaking with a few of the regulars, the obsession theme seemed to crop up time and again. Orient, and I'm sure the same could be said of most lower-league clubs, seem to attract the anorak fans – the ones whose very existence is defined by the club. They regard Premier League football snobbishly, as something only the dim-witted would enjoy, while their own particular league is a purist's pursuit. I was beginning to see why real ale was so popular in the Supporters Club. I was a Spurs fans who wanted regular, honest football at a local club and had become tired with the Premier League, so where did that place me on the football fan spectrum? Dim-wit or anorak? Would I develop a taste for real ale too?

Orient started playing some decent passing football at last and although Huddersfield were standing firm, there were some signs of a recovery. They were quashed in the 78th minute when a shot from Huddersfield's Jordan Rhodes took a wicked deflection and found its way into the bottom corner of the Orient net.

Another defeat loomed large, but straight from the kick-off the ball was launched forward by centre-back Ben Chorley. Alex Revell met it at the edge of the box and cushioned a header across goal into the path of Dean Cox. Striding onto it, Cox hit a volley with the outside of his right boot, sending a 25-yard curling shot into the top corner of the net.

From behind the goal we watched the move unfold and leapt into the air in delight as the ball flew past the despairing arm of the Huddersfield keeper. An absolute cracker of a goal! The momentum of the game shifted. 2-1 down, Orient were now pressing hard, and for the remaining ten minutes the visitors did all they could to hang on to their slender lead.

Disappointingly, the shrill peep of the referee's final whistle halted a resurgent Orient in their tracks and groans of frustration filled the air. We stood and gave the players a huge round of applause. They had lost, but showed real fight. Often that means more to fans than anything else.

Now a few games into the season, we began to recognise the little traits and characteristics of certain players. Matt Spring was too slow in our opinion. Elliot Omozusi wasn't intelligent and got caught out of position too often. 36-year-old Scott McGleish was past it.

We all walked back to the tube together discussing these insights and trailing behind a group of loud and obnoxious away fans. They were shouting and pushing each other around, one even stepped in the road and held up traffic, pointing at a young mother in her car and shouting 'YOU, DON'T FOOKIN' MOVE.'

'What a bunch o'wankers!' Murph said, staring at them with a look of distaste on his face so pronounced it looked like he'd drunk some of my lime cordial at the Supporters Club. Before the match, I had admired the away fans' fun and jovial spirit. Now I was sickened by their boisterousness. It's funny how one result can put a different spin on things.

We didn't have another Orient home match for almost two weeks. In the meantime, I had the opening game of Spurs' Champions League group stage to enjoy. Unfortunately it was on a Tuesday night, which meant it was on Sky Sports, something I didn't have. In much the same way as I dislike going to football matches on my own, the alternative of standing in a busy pub and watching the game on TV in solitude was even worse. Thankfully, if you know where to look online, the game is streamed live, although the Chinese commentary can be a bit of a distraction.

Before the game started I received an excited phone call from Murph. It turned out former Arsenal youth full-back Kerrea Gilbert was playing for Orient in a reserve game that same evening. This could be big news for the O's. He was a quality right-back and could be just what Orient needed. Murph filled me in on his Arsenal career and we talked about what it could mean for the club.

On the laptop's somewhat jerky live feed of the game at Werder Bremen, I watched in disbelief as Spurs burst into an early 2-0 lead. They were carving the Germans apart with neat and intricate passing and aggressive counter-attacking football. They had taken to the Champions League like ducks to water. I still remained pessimistic. I watched Spurs too often to get excited about things as impressive as a 2-0 lead in Germany. Chances were we would mess it up. Strangely, I was yet to be infected by the pessimism bug at Brisbane Road. 1-0 down? No problem, we'll get it back.

Was it because it was all so new at Orient? Was my heart still care-free and untroubled like a lovesick teenager? Was I yet to have my heart broken as Spurs had done to me on so many occasions? Or perhaps I didn't yet care enough, or I didn't feel personally attached to my new club.

Right on cue, Spurs shrank back into themselves. It was as if they had woken from a dream and realised where they were. 2-0 became 2-2 remarkably quickly, and the game ended with Spurs hanging on for a draw.

The O's poor form continued away from home. A 3-2 defeat at Notts County left them second from bottom and Russell Slade's tenure as manager was precariously in the balance. Chas, Murph and myself all agreed that they shouldn't do anything as rash as sack Slade less than ten games into the season. We had a big game against Brentford on Friday night, and that match was beginning to look like a make-or-break game for Slade.

Chas and Murph also made time to rub my nose in Spurs' 4-1 loss in extra time to Arsenal in the Carling Cup. In truth I wasn't that bothered. Both sides fielded reserve and youth players, showing how much they respected the competition, so their taunts and jokes didn't even register a response. Three points on Friday mattered more to me at this moment in time.

<u>Friday 24th September 2010</u>
<u>Orient v Brentford</u>

Rain and wind swept over London. The game kicked off at 7:45pm, and before then I had half a day off to play in my company's charity five-a-side tournament. Competition was a bit thin on the ground, with only five teams turning out. With the weather the way it was, it was a surprise anyone bothered to show up at all.

The tournament was scaled down to a five-team league format with the top two playing a final once all the other games had been completed. Our team had a good mixture of skill and stamina, with the advantage of 6' 3" tall Kevin between the posts. In my experience, having a decent goalkeeper is essential to five-a-side success. Sure enough, our campaign got off to a fine start, winning 6-0, 1-0 and 5-1 in our opening games. Our only blemish was a 3-1 defeat to a side that basically kicked, pushed and hacked their way through the entire twelve-minute match. It put us entirely off our game plan and we resorted to similar tactics in frustration as they brushed us aside and topped the group. Justice was served when we faced them in the final. In a close game we came out 2-0 winners and I opened the scoring. It was my first football trophy since I was 16.

Over beers afterwards it turned out that our goalkeeper was a West Ham fan, but he was as disillusioned with the Premier League, and football in general, as I was.

'I used to go to Upton Park every week with my dad and brother,' he revealed as we sat in the spitting rain sipping our pints. 'It was when Tevez and Mascherano signed for us that I gave up on it all. No one at the club seemed to care that they were losing every game and were bottom of the league. It was too expensive, I couldn't sit with my family anymore, so I sacked it off.'

It seemed I wasn't the only one feeling this way about modern football, and I didn't even go week-in week-out like Kevin had done. He had more to turn his back on, and he did so grudgingly, but there is a limit to every fan's patience.

I dashed back home to get showered and changed – being careful to display my shiny new prize in front of the TV for Stace to fawn over when she got home from work – and set off for Brisbane Road.

I met Chas and Murph, who had just returned from a business-related tour of Newcastle's St James' Park, and we went straight to the ground, stopping for a pie and a beer before we took our seats. Five games of five-a-side should surely balance out the pastry and pint calorie consumption for one evening. Jamie was living it up in Ibiza for a week and probably had no idea there was a match on.

Brentford had beaten Everton on penalties in the Carling Cup in midweek and everyone was hoping for a cup hangover to affect them this evening. Orient chairman Barry Hearn had been on the TV talking positively about the club's plight. He was 'under no illusions about the situation' but made it clear that Slade was safe in his job – the dreaded vote of coinfidence that meant that the manager was hanging on by a thread.

Despite the Kerrea Gilbert trial coming to nothing, Orient had completed the loan signing of Spurs youngster Paul-Jose M'Poku a few days previously and the Belgian winger was among the substitutes. Could he provide that little spark of invention? The exuberance of youth often had that effect. As it was, he remained glued to the subs bench.

The game was scruffy and scrappy. Having lost the last three at home, nerves were tight both in the stands and on the pitch. We relaxed a little after 25 minutes when McGleish smashed the ball home and ran off to celebrate with the jubilant crowd.

As the game wore on, it became a battle of wills between the Orient defence and Brentford attack as set piece after set piece was floated dangerously into the box. Chas was rocking back and forwards anxiously in his seat. He had yet to witness an Orient win this season, having missed the excitement of the Exeter game. It seemed a long time ago to me, too.

The final whistle was a merciful rescue after another late assault from the visitors. Slade punched the air in delight and the players, looking as relieved as the crowd, came over to show us their appreciation.

'He's here, he's there, he's every-fucking-where, Scott McGleish, Scott McGleish,' the crowd sang as the goal scorer ran over to join his team mates. For tonight at least, he was the star.

<u>Tuesday 28th September 2010</u>
<u>Orient v Walsall</u>

Tottenham's start to the league season was as unconvincing as Orient's. They suffered defeat at Premier League strugglers and London rivals West Ham. I watched the scores on *Soccer Saturday*, my pessimism with Spurs again showing no bounds as I was sure they had no chance of an equaliser. Yet by the evening I had forgotten about it. Stace noted this with considerable pleasure, it was a far cry from the days where my whole weekend and most of the next week would be doom and gloom if Spurs lost. Murph said much the same after Arsenal lost the following Tuesday. Perhaps we were maturing at last?

Never mind doom and gloom, the following week was pure contentment. With plenty of annual leave to take at work, I'd decided to have the week off so Stace and I could enjoy some pleasant coupley activities like walks around Hever Castle in Kent and afternoon tea.

Tuesday night, however, was Orient night. Fellow strugglers Walsall were arriving off the back of a 2-1 defeat at the weekend, setting up what was already a relegation six-pointer early in the season. I was running late having spent longer on a shopping trip negotiating the crowds on Oxford Street than I would have liked. Bloody tourists.

Jamie returned from his hedonistic adventures in the Balearics and completed our regular foursome, which had been less than regular these past weeks. We were yet to see Orient win when all four of us were present. With the season almost two months old, that was a sad indictment of Orient's poor form as much as of our attendance.

Orient and Walsall played out a dire 0-0 game that was punctuated by half chances and poor passing throughout. We spent the majority of the game talking about Chas and Jamie's love lives. Chas was no longer seeing his Jordanian-Iranian sweetheart, having been spotted by her when he pulled a different girl in a club the night before. Jamie had taken a shine to a Brazilian stripper he met in a club down the Hackney Road. He'd taken her out on a few dates but hadn't sealed the deal because he felt it was inappropriate. For all Jamie's promiscuity, it was ironic that it had taken a stripper to make him think about his decorum.

The temperature had dropped, reminding us all what lay ahead in the coming months. I needed to find myself a suitable coat to protect myself from a wintry onslaught in the smaller Brisbane Road stands.

The end of the month saw Spurs play their first Champions League group stage match at White Hart Lane against Dutch champions FC Twente. As I was still technically on holiday and having been at the Orient game the previous night, I decided I would ignore the football for the evening so Stace and I could go out and enjoy a nice meal and a film. It also helped circumvent the inevitable argument that was bound to occur had I said I was stopping in to watch the game on a tiny laptop monitor.

I tried to ignore the game as best I could when I got home, hoping to avoid the score and catch the highlights. Curiosity got the better of me. I flicked the live game on, Valencia against Manchester United. There were no updates from White Hart Lane, so I waited. I waited some more. I left it as long as I could, making it to full-time, then couldn't wait any longer. In the same way people rip off a sticking plaster, I closed my eyes, flicked the channel over to Sky Sports News and then opened them in a flash... 4-1! Get in! Settling back in my seat, I relaxed and waited for what would be some enjoyable highlights. If only Orient could bang in four goals too.

```
17.Southampton.........P9 |W2 |D3 |L4 |F7 |A8 |9pts
18.Tranmere Rovers.....P9 |W2 |D3 |L4 |F8 |A14|9pts
19.Hartlepool United...P9 |W2 |D3 |L4 |F8 |A16|9pts
20.Leyton Orient.......P9 |W2 |D2 |L5 |F10|A13|8pts
21.Yeovil Town.........P9 |W2 |D2 |L5 |F10|A18|8pts
22.Walsall.............P9 |W2 |D1 |L6 |F10|A14|7pts
23.Dagenham&Redbridge..P9 |W1 |D4 |L4 |F9 |A16|7pts
```

October 2010

Tuesday 5th October 2010
Orient v Brentford

Only eleven days since the league win over Brentford, the Bees returned to Brisbane Road for the second round of the Johnstone's Paint Trophy. It hadn't been a good day at the office. After much deliberation and heart-wrenching discussion, no doubt over champagne buffets and lobster dinners, it had been decided by the powers-that-be that my department was to be put under review for the potential outsourcing of our work. As much as I disliked what I did, a job was a job and losing it was not something I had bargained for. We were told we would have to go through a series of pilot programs to see how efficiently our work practices could be done by people in the Far East. I wasn't surprised, for some time I had an inkling that this eventuality would rear its ugly head, but it didn't make the reality of the situation any easier to take and I needed some cheering up. Hopefully the O's would oblige.

With the economic climate the way it was and people watching every penny – something I would have to start doing in light of recent events – financing low-key mid-week cup fixtures was pretty low on the list of essential expenditures. It was no surprise that the Supporters Club was virtually deserted when I arrived. The club, knowing full well that the turnout was going to be poor, had reduced ticket prices to £10 and closed off most of the ground. We were evicted from our usual seats and relocated to the West Stand.

Jamie and Chas were late as usual, so Murph and I stood outside enjoying the autumnal warmth that was likely to give way to bitter cold any day now. We struck up a conversation with an Irishman who was a regular at Brisbane Road. Like Murph and Chas, his first allegiance was to Arsenal. He told us that when he first came to London he lived in Highbury and went every week to watch the Gunners play. It was the same old story though, as the prices went up the traditional support began to fall away and he could no longer afford to make regular visits.

'I still go occasionally,' he said, taking a sip of his pint. 'I've got friends who can get me tickets whenever I want but they cost me £60 a go. And that's before you buy a programme, something to eat and a couple of drinks. I'm glad I don't have a couple of nippers to take along too. I'd be bankrupt in no time. It's a rich man's game now, sure enough.'

We stood chatting to him about our reasons for coming to watch Orient and the ways in which the club could attract more fans like us until kick-off approached. With no sign of Jamie or Chas, we went through the turnstiles and found our seats a few rows from the pitch to the right of the away dugout.

Only a thousand or so had turned out for the game. The stand opposite was dark and deserted. The famous white dormer stuck out of the roof, its red-lettered 'Leyton Orient' sign stood out brightly against the darkening sky. To our right were the empty seats of the Tommy Johnston Stand. The word 'ORIENT' was spelled out in white across the otherwise blood-red bank of seats and we could see where we usually sat despite the veil of shadow cast across them from the roof above. Mine, I deduced, was at the top of the second vertical line of the 'N'. It felt foreign sitting elsewhere, and with the subdued atmosphere, I wasn't feeling at all up for the match.

Jamie arrived and immediately asked how long the game would go on for if it was a draw.

'Have you got somewhere else to be mate?' I asked.

'Well, yeah, I've been seeing this Swedish bird for a while and she said she'd cook me dinner.'

'What the hell are you doing here then you mug?' I laughed. 'This is going to be a rubbish game and you've got meatballs and who knows what else waiting for you somewhere across town!'

He shrugged his shoulders. 'I'm sure she'll keep them warm for me. So does this go to extra time and penalties or what?'

We had no idea, which left Jamie grumbling and looking impatiently at his watch as if this inconvenience was in some way our fault.

The game kicked off, still with no sign of Chas, and from the outset it was clear that it was going to be a long night. It wasn't just me that wasn't in the mood. Neither side seemed like they wanted to be there, the managers appeared to be paying lip service to their usual duties of shouting and pointing, and the fans didn't seem to be paying much attention to what was happening on the pitch. Chas finally arrived as the game neared half-time, took his seat and began explaining his lateness to the others. As usual I was stuck at the end of the row and couldn't hear a word they were saying.

At half-time we headed inside for refreshment. Unsure of what I fancied, I scanned the options on the board. Murph turned from the counter with his hands wrapped tightly around a steaming cardboard cup.

'What did you go for mate? Tea?' I asked, peering down through the steam.

'No, it's Bovril,' he replied, blowing a jet of cool air over the top of the cup and sending a cloud of vapour in all directions.

'What is Bovril?' I asked. 'I always thought it was like a cup of gravy or something.'

'It's a beef drink. Proper tasty and warms you right up. Here, have a sip.'

I cautiously put my lips to the edge of the cup, conscious that whatever lay within was scalding hot, and took a careful sip. A meaty and salty beef flavour filled my mouth and the warmth of the liquid as it slid down my throat was a welcome pleasure after the early mildness of the evening's temperature had been lost to a creeping chill.

'Oooh, that's a treat that is!' I said, handing the cup back to its owner. 'It's just a cup of hot beef stock. So simple. I'm getting one!'

Settling back into our seats, all clutching a piping hot cup of liquid meat, the game got back underway and picked up where it had left off in the first half. The one bright spot in the game was young Paul-Jose M'poku, the Spurs loanee. His direct running and eagerness to take on the full-back grabbed everyone's attention. Slade had put him on the left of midfield and at every opportunity the young Belgian would skip inside, drop his shoulder, beat the first man and make a bee-line for the next defender. He had flicks, step-overs and a turn of pace that was terrifying the retreating Brentford defenders. It was great to watch, which was more than can be said for the rest of the game. The referee blew for full-time and the players trooped over to their respective dugouts. After a few minutes both goalkeepers emerged and headed to the goal to our left.

'Must be going straight to penalties,' Murph said as he turned to Jamie, who punched the air in delight and pulled out his phone to fire off a quick heads-up message to his Scandinavian dinner date.

In the history of watching football, both on TV and in the flesh, I have never witnessed my team win a penalty shootout. I missed the England victory against Spain in 1996, the only time they have won a tie on penalties. They are a cruel way to end a game of football and it often makes a villain out of an individual, but there is something uniquely dramatic about a penalty shootout. Man against man, one chance – who picks the right spot, who holds their nerve? After a frankly turgid game, my pulse rate quickened as a Brentford player stepped up to make the first attempt.

After nine perfectly-taken spot kicks, the score was 5-4 to Brentford. Matt Spring was up next for the O's in what was essentially a sudden death kick. Score and we continue, miss and we go home. He strode forward, tossing the ball up once into the air and catching it, before placing it carefully on the spot. He turned, took a few strides back and faced the goalkeeper. The ref blew the whistle. He jogged forward and side-footed it to the keeper's right. The keeper dived and saved it.

There was a collective sigh of disappointment from the 900 Orient fans, all of whom got to their feet in unison and made for the exit. The small pocket of about 100 Bees supporters behind the goal cheered and the players ran forward to congratulate the victorious keeper. My poor penalty shootout record continued.

<u>Saturday 16th October 2010</u>
<u>Orient v Hartlepool United</u>

Now that the cruel hand of rendundancy was hovering over my employment status, waiting to swat me like a fly, it's fair to say the mood in the office was at an all-time low. Like condemned men asked to tie their own nooses, we were charged with overseeing and guiding our would-be replacements, thousands of miles away in Manila, as they attempted to get to grips with our roles.

To further complicate matters, Stace had chosen to leave her full-time job at the gallery and go part-time so she could concentrate on her new art business and get some freelance make-up jobs. As nervous as she was about making such a big step, and despite losing almost half her income, I insisted she was doing the right thing. The timing was not perfect, but if we could read crystal balls, we'd never leave the bookies. Besides, I wasn't unemployed yet, so the bills and the rent were being paid and all was well.

In a stroke of rare good fortune, Stace was asked to do the make-up on the TV entertainment leviathan The X Factor. From now until Christmas, all her time at the weekend would be spent backstage applying make-up to wannabe pop stars. Despite the obvious disadvantage of her not being around on weekends when I wasn't at the football, it did mean that there would be no arguments or ill-feeling about me disappearing off to Brisbane Road every other Saturday. It also meant I didn't have to sit through the bloody programme every Saturday and Sunday evening, so for those two reasons, I could have given Simon Cowell a big sloppy kiss.

With Stace off rubbing shoulders with the nearly-famous on her first Saturday at the live show, I was back to Leyton for the visit of Hartlepool. I had miraculously recovered from a debilitating case of man flu which had kept me off work the previous day and I rose from my sick bed to find clear blue skies. Feeling chipper and in the mood for a few pints, I made my way across Brick Lane, past Spitalfields Market and down to the underground at Liverpool Street. A big sign greeted me: 'Due to engineering works the Central Line will not be running between Liverpool Street and Leytonstone.'

Piss, fuck, bollocks! I stood silently cursing Transport for London, Boris Johnson and anyone else I could think of who could possibly be blamed for this ball-ache of a predicament. Thankfully I had left early, the plan being to meet at the Supporters Club at 1pm, so I turned on my heels and walked quickly across Bishopsgate, down through Devonshire Square and over to Aldgate East station. My idea was to get the District Line to Barking and the Overground to Leyton Midland Road and walk the rest of the way. It was a mission, but a necessary one. After waiting a quarter of an hour on the platform at Aldgate East, I was forced to wait a further 40 minutes at Barking for a train heading towards Gospel Oak. I only wanted to go four stops! Eventually, after a further 20-minute walk from Leyton Midland Road station, I arrived at the ground a mere one hour and fifteen minutes later than planned. With barely enough time to have the pint I thoroughly deserved, we headed to our seats.

Jamie was missing again, having gone up to Scotland to visit family. He was replaced by Joss, the husband of Murph's fiancée's best friend, a short, jovial chap with deep-set eyes and an impish grin. He was a Sunderland fan, born and raised in the nearby city of Durham, which meant that although he had a typical north-east brogue, he considered it an insult if you called him a Geordie.

'See ya cannae call me Geordie cos I'm not from New-cassell!' he insisted when we raised the subject.

'I can't understand a word of what you just said,' Murph joked as Chas attempted an imitation of Joss's accent by uttering broken phrases from nineties children's TV series Byker Grove.

'Ah, ya bunch o' soft south'n, shandy drink'n bastards!' Joss joked back, grinning.

Hartlepool had brought a good level of travelling support and they were making some noise over to our right.

'You want to be careful what you say here Joss,' I said, biting into a hot dog and dripping mustard down my jumper. 'They'll think you're an away fan!'

'Aye,' he said, 'me dad's from Hartlepool as it happens. Funny that I come here today when the Munkee Hangas were playing wasn't it?'

'Monkey Hangers?' I asked, looking puzzled.

'Aye, it's what they call people from Hartlepool. Dates back tae Napoleonic times'.

Joss went on to explain the full story. Local folklore tells a tale of when a French warship was wrecked off the coast of Hartlepool. The only surviving member of the crew was a monkey that the crew had dressed, presumably for their own amusement, as a French sailor. Not knowing what a Frenchman looked like, or even what a monkey was, the locals held a trial on the beach. With the captive creature unable or unwilling to answer their questions, they presumed it was a French spy and summarily hung the poor beast from the mast of a fishing boat.

With roars of laughter from the rest of us, Joss finished his story. 'I dinnae know if it's true like, but that's why we call 'em Munkee Hangas. They even have a munkee mascot called H'Angus too. He was elected mayor of Hartlepool a couple o' times.'

The game started with us still chuckling and shaking our heads with incredulity. The laughter died away pretty quickly as the game turned into a never-ending series of misplaced passes and poor control. The sun had gone in and the sky clouded over. The fans around us were getting increasingly restless and frustrated. As the half-time whistle blew, a few boos followed the departing players off the field.

Behind us, Paul, the fan responsible for much of the singing, took great umbrage with one old boy for his negative reaction.

'What kind of fan are you!' he shouted.

'I'm supposed to applaud that?' the old guy shot back.

He wasn't wrong. The performance had so far been terrible. It made me wonder what fans expected from their teams at this level of the game. Should Orient or Hartlepool be passing the ball fluidly and playing like Barcelona? What is the standard that League One clubs aspire to reach? Perhaps the cost of a match ticket is linked to the expectations of a fan? It's impossible to compare, but I wonder whether a few decades ago it was easier for a supporter to take a bad game if they'd only spent a few quid on it. It's not overly expensive in League One, but £20 is still a fair amount to shell out on a game. Is it the case that, faced with rising prices throughout the league pyramid, supporters now expect more bang for their buck?

The second half was much better. Slade decided to bring on M'poku just ten minutes after the interval, replacing the unusually-poor Dean Cox who had started to show his frustration with some bad challenges. The change was almost instant. Faced with the onrushing M'poku, the Hartlepool defence began to back off, and by the time he'd left his third victim flat on his backside, they looked downright petrified whenever he got the ball.

With time running out and Hartlepool's defence standing firm, M'poku lined up a free kick. Somehow he embarrassingly fluffed it, but it took a deflection and went out for a corner. Charlie Daniels whipped the ball in, and with Hartlepool failing to clear the ball from the danger area, another of Orient's substitutes, Jonathan Téhoué, pounced on the loose ball. A square patch of empty and unguarded net opened up in front of our eyes, the only real glimpse of goal the Hartlepool rear guard had exposed all day, and Téhoué lashed the ball home in that exact spot.

The home crowd erupted. The tension and anxiety seemed to have built up so much pressure around the ground, and as the ball hit the net it was as though some-one had hit the release valve. 'I like Téhoué-houé, I like Téhoué-houé, I like Téhoué-houé, you like Te-houé,' the crowd sang to the tune of the nineties dance hit 'I Like to Move it'.

After a few pints in the Supporters Club, we walked up to Leytonstone tube station in high spirits to continue the celebrations at The George in South Woodford. With Jamie absent, we still hadn't been able to enjoy a victory when the four of us had been present, but Joss had been our north-eastern good luck charm and a worthy stand-in. Chas, Murph and I suggested he came more often when we realised that it was the first time Orient, Tottenham and Arsenal all won on the same day. It was a very suc-cessful weekend, which made getting up early on Sunday with a splitting headache for a round of golf with my brother-in-law that much more bearable. It didn't help my golf swing though.

Back in the world of work, the ridiculous nature of our department's predicament continued. In a shameless display of corporate bullshit, a half-day meeting in a con-ference suite near the Tower of London announced that after eighteen months of troubled times and hardship, the management was pleased to announce that there would be no more redundancies. They neglected to mention that the department I was in was still under scrutiny and we were only in the second week of a three-month outsourcing pilot. There was a big cheer, a round of applause, and a buffet and free drinks were laid on afterwards. Amidst disgruntled conversations with my colleagues, I duly took full advantage of the free refreshments and then headed quickly home to enjoy Spurs play Inter Milan at the San Siro on TV.

This was what Champions League was about – big nights at big stadia against big clubs. This time Spurs were up against the reigning European champions. Having no Sky Sports, I began the usual trawl of the internet for a suitable live stream. As soon as the buffering and loading completed, Spurs were a goal behind. The Italians carved Spurs open and the oldest player on the pitch, Javier Zanetti, fired past a helpless Heurelho Gomes inside three minutes. It got worse just minutes later. Gomes, scrambling to narrow the angle on an approaching Inter player, brought him down. He was shown a red card and Samuel Eto'o duly dispatched the penalty to make it 2-0. By half-time it was all over. Inter were four goals to the good and Spurs, playing with ten men, looked completely out of their depth.

'Ha ha Spurs are shit!'

'Champions League? You're having a laugh!'

Mocking text messages were pouring in. In the end I turned my phone off and slumped back into the sofa cushions for a sulk. Just a few minutes into the second half, Tottenham's young winger Gareth Bale scored a consolation goal which I celebrated with an ironic little cheer. In the final minute, with the result beyond doubt, Bale broke down the left, cut inside and smashed a low drive past Julio Cesar in the Inter goal. I sat up and applauded what was a scintillating run and finish. Seconds later, déjà vu, Bale burst through again and smashed the ball past Cesar into the corner of the net. There was no time left, so it finished 4-3 to Inter with a Bale hat-trick.

What a finish to the game! After a dire first half, this was a real boost for Spurs. Inter sat back a little when they were four goals up and they were entitled to take it a bit easy, but it was nice to see Spurs get some pride back. Losing 4-3 away to the European Champions was not a shameful result. This Champions League season was proving to be interesting.

I had kept a close eye on Spurs' Champions League campaign, but the vagaries of the Premier League had largely passed me by. I found myself drawn back into its murky, over-financed world when news broke that Wayne Rooney wanted to leave Manchester United. Out of the blue, Rooney announced he was unwilling to sign a new contract and wanted to quit the club. Merely days later, after death threats and protests outside his house and with Alex Ferguson saying that he was resigned to his star striker leaving, Rooney put pen to paper on a five-year deal worth in the region of £180,000 per week. The whole story seemed to be about Rooney and Ferguson – or more accurately, their agents and accountants – posturing and trying to get the best deal.

In one of football's great paradoxes, Portsmouth held a press conference on the same day that Rooney signed the deal to make him one of the highest paid players in the Premier League. The south coast club had been in administration for some time and called the media to Fratton Park to announce that they could be liquidated if an agreement could not be reached between previous owner Alexander Gaydamak and prospective buyer Balram Chainrai.

The whole affair brought the reality of football's wage gulf into stark clarity. Ten years ago the average wage for a Premier League footballer was in the region of £9,000 per week. A decade on and that figure has more than doubled to £22,000 per week, or a pre-tax income of £1.1 million every year. This is before any sponsorship or endorsement money that big brands are willing to stump up to have their product pictured alongside a grinning player. In League One, just two promotions away from the Premier League, the average wage is around £1,400 per week or £73,000 per year. A division below that, in League Two, it's half that. £73,000 per year is a very healthy salary – several times that of the national average – but footballers have short careers and there are only so many coaching roles and managerial positions available after retirement.

It's no wonder players like Scott McGleish play well into their late thirties.

Perhaps it is unfair to compare averages in such a way. Football is entertainment after all, and in the same way an actor on Eastenders gets paid less than their Hollywood blockbuster counterpart, the gulf in class and ability is reflected in the pay packets. But where do we draw the line of what is an acceptable amount of money for someone to be paid to play football? Have we already crossed it? It made no sense to me that a club like Manchester United, who were mired in £600 million of debt, could afford to spend almost £10 million a year on a single player while another club carrying less debt could almost vanish from existence.

Back in the real world, despite Orient's slight improvement in results if not performance, it was a return to disappointment as the O's contrived to throw away 1-0 and 2-1 leads to draw away at ten-man Swindon. The result meant that Orient sat 20th in League One, but they were still just six points behind eighth place. This division was proving to be a level playing field with every team capable of beating everyone else, and the points tallies were so compacted that a few wins in a row could shoot a club up the table. Conversely, a few sour results and they would sink like a stone. Hopefully Orient had been through their worst, so onwards and upwards!

The draw for the first round of the FA Cup occurred on a Sunday while Stace was off at The X Factor. Similarly to the Johnstone's Paint Trophy, the first round of the FA Cup was something that usually passed under my Spurs-supporting radar. It happened at the end of a day during which I sat watching match after match of football through whatever medium I could find, and in some cases had two games running at the same time, cable TV and internet streaming working to its fullest. In one afternoon I managed to take in Parma v Roma, Celtic v Rangers, PSV v Feyenoord, Bayer Leverkusen v Mainz, Man City v Arsenal, Man United v Stoke and Inter v Sampdoria. At the conclusion of those games and the bucket-load of goals (including PSV beating their fierce rivals Feyenoord 10-0), Orient drew Dagenham and Redbridge away in the FA Cup. A chance for revenge after the league defeat perhaps, although I didn't fancy a second tour of 'Nam so soon after the first.

Saturday 30th October 2010
Orient v Rochdale

The ominous clatter of the redundancy bandwagon rumbled closer. During the week I received a letter from my boss who reluctantly informed me that several of my core duties were to be reallocated around the rest of the editorial department. This essentially meant that, from now on, I was on borrowed time. It also meant work would be ridiculously quiet, even more so than usual. More time to research and plan the weekend, then.

The Rochdale fixture had been earmarked by Orient as Community Day. Every season ticket holder was entitled to one free ticket for a friend or family member to enjoy a day at Brisbane Road. We decided this was a perfect chance to get the boys along who, like cowards, did not follow through on their promises made at the Leeds game the season before. This was an opportunity to show them what they were missing.

Bad news came crashing in when we found out Chas, who had been complaining about back problems for a while, had gone into hospital for an operation and would be absent from Brisbane Road for the foreseeable future. We had recently booked a lads weekend in Portugal to watch Benfica, but the poor old lummox would have to miss that as well. He was understandably down in the dumps, so we promised him we would try not to have too much fun until he returned.

My cousins from Scotland were down in London so I'd been whisked off on an impromptu piss-up around north London, the highlight of which was seeing a Jägerbomb (Jägermeister and Red Bull) thrust into my 61-year-old dad's hand and watching him drain the glass in one.

I was feeling somewhat jaded (or should that be Jägered) as I made my way over to Liverpool Street on Saturday morning to meet some mates before we headed over to Leyton. Foulser was already waiting for me outside the Hamilton Hall pub. His wife was due to give birth in less than a month and this was likely to be the last time we went out on the lash together before fatherhood pinned him down.

'Nick's running late and the dickhead has left his phone at home,' he said to me as we shook hands.

We didn't have long to wait for our missing man as Nick soon appeared around the corner. He'd seen an advert about a hair specialist in Victoria who could put in hair implants and had taken them up on their kind offer of a free consultation. Nick was receding faster than a high tide, something that his debauched lifestyle was contributing to. In the past he had been known to smash watermelons on his head, have colonic irrigation and disrobe in public, so hair restoration was about as normal as he got.

We arrived at Leyton Station just after 1:30pm and met the others. Our full complement was three regulars – Murph, Jamie and I – together with our guests – Foulser, Nick, Cads and Chelsea fan Liam. I could already tell this was going to be a cracking day.

We congregated outside the Supporters Club, enjoying the atmosphere and the pre-match banter, supping pints and catching up on the latest bizarre incidents that Nick had managed to get himself involved with. The Community Day free tickets were proving extremely popular as beyond the doors, inside the club, the bar was heaving with people.

A young guy approached us holding a clipboard. 'Afternoon gents, I'm with Sky TV. Is anyone interested in doing a football quiz after the game today?'

Before I'd even had a chance to compute what the bloke had said, Liam leaned forward stuck a finger in my chest. 'He'll do it.'

'Err, yeah, I suppose... why not?' I spluttered.

'Great, can I take your name and number?'

I had a sudden jolt of alarm. 'They won't be Orient questions will they?'

'Are you not an Orient fan?'

'Well, yeah, I am... but I'm kind of new.'

Having only been a part of the club for a matter of months and knowing very little about its history, I didn't feel ready to go on national television and purport to be an Orient fan only to be ritually humiliated by scoring zero points on the topic I was supposed to know inside out.

'No, don't worry, they're just general football questions,' he replied, helping to quell the knot that had started to tighten in my gut.

Slightly bewildered at the unusual turn the day had taken, I gave him my details and turned back to the group. Murph volunteered his details too, and after letting us know what to do and where to go at full-time, the researcher disappeared through the crowd of bodies.

With kick-off fast approaching, we finished our pints and made our way to our seats. Wanting to avoid stains for my screen debut, I avoided the usual hot dog or pie lunch. The others tucked in anyway; Nick demolished two hot dogs in quick succession.

With close to 5,000 fans filling the seats around the ground, the noise on all sides was noticeably louder. Unfortunately for the fans in attendance, the match failed to live up to the atmosphere. Rochdale were in the ascendency early on, but despite dominating the possession and carving out one or two openings, Lee Butcher in the Orient goal remained untroubled. That was until we got up from our seats to beat the half-time rush for a pint. As we approached the door to the bar, we heard a muted cheer. Rochdale had taken the lead.

I wasn't sure whether it was nerves or the half-time score that soured my beer, but after an unpleasant pint of lager, I retreated back to my seat before the lads had finished. It turned out to be a wise move. Soon after the game got back under way, Orient went on the offensive. As Dean Cox burst into the box, a Rochdale defender came across to close him down. Making the most of minimal contact, the little winger tumbled to the floor, arms splayed. The referee gave a sharp peep of his whistle and pointed to the spot, much to the amusement of the crowd in the Tommy Johnston Stand. Of all the penalty shouts we'd had that season, today's official had awarded us the least obvious. As the rest of the lads reappeared and retook their seats, Ben Chorley stepped up and coolly slotted the ball past the Rochdale keeper.

Now on the front foot and buoyed by a vociferous crowd, Orient pressed on. In the 66th minute they turned the game on its head. Matt Spring combined well with skipper Stephen Dawson, who sent Cox clear. He scampered towards the onrushing keeper and stroked the ball under his despairing glove and into the net.

Rochdale had no response and for the remaining 25 minutes Orient looked comfortable. The full-time whistle completed the day's work for the players, but mine was just about to begin. My nerves returned with a vengeance.

Murph, Jamie and I waited at the foot of the stairs that led to pitch level while the rest of the lads went to the Supporters Club. The chap with the Sky clipboard came to find us.

'We're only going to need one of you I'm afraid lads,' he said apologetically, 'but I'll give £20 to whoever doesn't do it to say thanks for turning up.'

'I'll go for that!' Murph said quickly, looking pleased. 'You put your name down first Ad, so it's only fair. You'll probably do better than me anyway!'

We walked up the stairs and along the edge of the pitch to where a small camera crew, a young blonde lady and a dark-haired man in a light-brown coat were standing near the halfway line. The players were warming down to our left, running sprints back and forward and stretching on the ground. This was all very surreal.

'Is that Charlotte Jackson?' Murph asked the clipboard guy. 'Chas is going to be gutted he missed this, he loves that bird!'

As we approached the crew, the dark-haired man stepped forward and introduced himself as Fenners from *Soccer AM*.

'So what's this all for then?' I asked Fenners.

'It's called 'Take It Like A Fan'. We ask you questions about football and the more you get right, the more cash you win. Have you not watched it before?' I shook my head. 'Does no-one bloody watch it anymore?' he sighed, turning to his film crew and looking mildly frustrated.

The cameraman took me to one side and began filming me close-up, manoeuvring his camera around my feet, up to my waist, into my face and onto the scarf that Murph had leant me for that bit of authenticity. Just as we were about to get underway, Charlie Daniels, Orient's left-back, shouted over as he was leaving the field.

'How many you gonna get?' he asked, waiting on the threshold of the tunnel.

'No idea, we'll see!' I replied, not quite knowing what to say.

'Well, good luck!' he shouted back.

'I'll do it for you Charlie,' I replied, inwardly cringing at my sycophantic response. Is TV meant to make you act like an idiot?

The camera rolled. With Murph and Jamie watching on, making quiet wisecracks, Fenners took me through the rules.

'This is Fenners Tenners! 60 seconds, every correct answer gets you ten quid, got it? Let's do it. Your time starts... now!'

'Where do Rochdale play?'

'Spotland.'

'How old is Diego Maradona?'

'Fifty.'

'What country does Peter Reid manage?'

'Errr... pass!'

'Thailand.'

'Who is the president of UEFA?'

'Platini.'

'Alex Ferguson's son manages which Championship side?'

'Preston.'

The minute flew by and I lost count of the amount I'd got right.

'Time's up. You got ten right!' Fenners said excitedly.

'Nice, that's a one-er!' I replied in my best East London accent.

'That's right, a one-er. One hundred pounds coming your way, if you want to take it.'

Charlotte Jackson reached forward and handed ten crisp bank notes to the host, who waved them tantalisingly close to my fingers.

'Do you want to take your hundred pounds or do you want to double-or-quits?'

'GAMBLE!' Murph cried from behind the camera.

'Well, Orient just won and got three points, it's been a good day... so I'm gonna take the money.'

He asked me the double-or-quits question anyway, which annoyingly I got right. But with the trip to Lisbon on the horizon, I thought that an extra £100 wasn't worth gambling away. I was more than happy with my afternoon's work as the glamorous Miss Jackson counted the money into my grateful hands.

Just as we were about to wrap up, Murph piped up. 'You know Peter Reid doesn't actually manage anyone at the moment? It's Bryan Robson that manages Thailand now.'

Fenners face dropped. He then spent the next few minutes effing and blinding and crouched down on his haunches deep in thought. 'We can't use it!' he said solemnly after rejoining the rest of us. 'You were so good as well, it's gutting. You're exactly the type of person we love having on the show and I don't think we can use it. I don't believe it!' He seemed genuinely apologetic.

'I can do it again if you want, and get the same questions right and wrong like I did before,' I suggested.

'Can't do it. It's not real then. It's got to be genuine,' he said, crouching back down again.

After a few minutes deliberation, they decided they would have to go and find someone else. Having been assured I could keep the money, I wasn't all that fussed about not being on the telly. As we were about to be led away from the pitch, the guy with the clipboard returned from the bar. Following close behind him was Cads, grinning widely.

'Cadman?' I laughed in disbelief. 'Of all the people in the bar you picked Cadman?' We roared with laughter. Cads' football knowledge, though not terrible, was limited to Liverpool Football Club.

A steward shepherded us from the touchline over towards the tunnel where a huddle of journalists surrounded

Russell Slade. Dean Cox, the match winner, was waiting patiently for his turn in front of the microphones.

'Coxy,' Murph said, 'can we get a quick photo with you?'

'Of course lads, no problem.'

With the steward protesting and insisting we leave, Cox strolled over, brushed past the steward and stood with us. The steward politely admitted defeat and held out his hand for our cameraphones. He guided us down the tunnel, past the steamy changing rooms where the laughing voices of the players echoed through the halls, and led us out onto Oliver Road next to the Supporters Club. We filled in the other lads on what happened.

With my new-found wealth and a large dose of peer pressure, I went to the bar and bought everyone a round of drinks. Cads returned with a respectable £50 and told everyone how his quiz had gone.

'They asked where Rochdale play. Well, I had no idea so I just said 'up north!''. We all laughed at what we knew was a typical Cads response, one that may well get air time.

The Orient captain, Stephen Dawson, came into the bar to enjoy a post-match beer with his family. With one Orient player already in the photo album, Murph and I added a second on the same day.

We stayed to watch Spurs play Man United at Old Trafford, a fixture that is historically unkind to the Lily-whites. Although United usually play Spurs off the park, controversies such as the Pedro Mendes disallowed goal in

2004 and numerous penalties that were given (to United) or not given (to Spurs) had left Spurs fans wondering whether the referee would ever let us win at Old Trafford again.

Tonight's game was no different. With United a goal to the good and Spurs looking threatening, Nani, United's young Portuguese winger, burst into the box and went down easily under a challenge. As he landed he stretched his hands out for the ball, only to be denied the penalty he thought he had won. Gomes, thinking the referee had given the free kick for hand ball, picked up the ball and rolled it a few yards in front of him as Nani got to his feet. Walking back past the Spurs goalkeeper, Nani looked up at the ref who shrugged his shoulders, prompting the United winger to turn and stroke the ball into the net. There was uproar and confusion as Spurs players surrounded the referee and linesman. With a flick of his arm, the ref turned from his assistant and signalled the goal.

As I stood watching the farcical scenes unfurl in front of my eyes, knowing full well this would rumble on in the press for days and days, I thought about the Orient match I'd just watched. The penalty that had got us back in the match was contentious, but with no video replays or forensic examination of every detail, there was nothing left to do but wait until the next fixture. That's how it should be. In a fairly-contested game you win some, you lose some.

With three points in the bag, a couple of pictures with the Orient players, new bank notes in my back pocket and a possible TV appearance on the cards, the scenes at Old Trafford, which would once have boiled my blood, paled into insignificance. It really didn't matter.

```
15.Brentford...........P14|W5 |D3 |L6 |F16|A17|18pts
16.Swindon Town........P14|W4 |D5 |L5 |F23|A24|17pts
17.Hartlepool United...P14|W4 |D5 |L5 |F14|A20|17pts
18.Leyton Orient.......P14|W4 |D4 |L6 |F16|A18|16pts
19.Notts County........P14|W5 |D1 |L8 |F19|A24|16pts
20.Tranmere Rovers.....P14|W4 |D4 |L6 |F17|A23|16pts
21.Plymouth Argyle.....P14|W4 |D4 |L6 |F17|A24|16pts
```

November 2010

The next fortnight's newspapers were filled with the controversy at Old Trafford, but I spent the time boring anyone who'd listen with the 'Take It Like A Fan' story. I suspected that I wouldn't make the final edit and my TV debut would be cast asunder on the cutting room floor after the cock-up they'd made with the Bryan Robson question. Instead, it would be Cadman's smiling visage peering back through our TV screens, not mine. I had seven days to wait to find out.

Tottenham's game against Inter Milan was coming up midweek, the same evening that Orient travelled away to Colchester. My football conscience was being tested. The glamour of the Champions League tie against the European Champions at White Hart Lane was intruding upon a vital league match for the O's. The lure of the big game was too strong, and I thought of nothing but the visit of the *Nerazzurri* for a couple of days.

The way Spurs finished the reverse fixture at the San Siro two weeks before made it seem as though they'd nicked a famous result, but the fact was they had lost the game. Were it not for a terrific hat-trick from Bale, it would have been a humiliation, something Spurs' rivals and critics were itching to rejoice over. Yet a win, however unlikely it seemed considering the hiding we took in the last meeting, would put us level on points at the top of the group, an incredible position to be in with two games to go. Realistically, I thought a draw was the best we could hope for.

Once again I found myself sat squinting at the pixelated, jerky images of a live internet feed owing to the fact that the game was being screened on Sky, not ITV. I had seen barely any of Spurs' adventures in Europe on a nice big television screen so far and was getting used to the eye strain and poor quality resolution the laptop offered.

The opening exchanges were as fluid a game of football as I had seen for some time. Tottenham were looking to break down the flanks at every opportunity, but the ever-present danger and movement from Samuel Eto'o and the creativity of Wesley Sneijder posed real problems for the Spurs defence.

It was Spurs' little Croatian, Luka Modric, who provided the spark that ignited the match. He threaded the ball perfectly to van der Vaart, who smashed the ball past the Inter keeper's near post and ran off towards the jubilant and writhing mass of supporters in the South Stand to celebrate.

The goal seemed to settle the players' nerves, and Gareth Bale in particular came into his own. Facing the Brazilian defender, Maicon, a player considered to be one of the best right-backs in the game, the young Welshman began a terrorising campaign of speed and agility down Spurs' left flank.

During the interval I turned the TV to Sky Sports News to see how Orient were getting on. Less well, it seemed. They had squandered a two-goal lead; Alex Revell scored two, only for Colchester to hit back before the end of the half with a couple for themselves. Curiosity satisfied, my attention turned back to north London with Spurs a goal to the good.

There was no let up from the men in white after the half-time break. Inter manager Rafael Benitez stood idly while his right-back was torn to shreds and Bale made his dominance count. Thundering past the backpedalling Brazilian for the umpteenth time, he fired a low ball across the face of goal and Peter Crouch, who had missed a sitter from a similar position in the first half, slid the ball comfortably into the net to make it 2-0. Two goals up against the champions of Europe – I was in ecstasy. The savaging continued as the crowd, whipped up by the Bale's magnificent performance, began taunting his beleaguered victim with chants of 'taxi for Maicon!'

With ten minutes to go, the Spurs faithful and I received a reminder that we were still watching Tottenham, a team proficient in snatching defeat from the jaws of victory. Samuel Eto'o, Inter's best performer on the night, cut in from the left hand side, dummied the ball past Alan Hutton and tucked it neatly past Carlo Cudicini. It was a wonderful goal, but it hit me like a brick.

I stopped bouncing excitedly in my seat and became very still. All the negative thoughts that had evolved during the years of watching Spurs throw leads away came flooding back like a tsunami. I panicked and hit the minimise button on the monitor. If I didn't watch, they would surely win. If I couldn't see it, it would all turn out OK. I wimped out. Ten nervy minutes in absolute ignorance was far better than seeing tragedy unfold in front of my eyes.

The minutes stretched into what seemed like hours and I became more and more anxious with every glance at my phone to see how long remained. In the end, I couldn't take the deafening silence. I flipped the laptop back open and clicked on the feed just in time to see Bale rocketing down the left again. Only a minute remained as he fired another perfect ball across the face of goal to an advancing Roman Pavlyuchenko, who knocked the ball in. With a shout of relief more than joy, I was up and celebrating around my front room. Stace poked her head out in bemusement from the bedroom where she'd taken refuge for the evening.

As the final whistle blew, I flicked to Sky Sports News to see the reaction to Tottenham's fine win. I was reminded, as the domestic scores scrolled slowly along the foot of the screen, that Orient were playing too. In all the excitement and panic of the second half, I completely forgot. Scanning the results, the final score struck me like a slap around the chops. Colchester had used the momentum of a two-goal comeback and nicked a winner in the 80th minute.

It was at this point that I reached the low in my Orient-supporting season. I wished I hadn't cashed in my chips and got rid of my Spurs membership in favour of the Orient season ticket. I had missed the chance to sit in White Hart Lane and see one of Spurs' all-time great results, while in the meantime Orient had thrown away what could, and probably should, have been a win.

Yet hindsight is a cruel and merciless mistress. Had I known in advance, would I have traded all the good times I'd had so far at Orient this season for one night of glory for Spurs? After a few moments of doubt, I realised that I wouldn't have done anything differently.

Having a second team to fall back on could serve as a nice pick-me-up. One can lift the mood when the other lets you down. Orient's victories, although few and far between so far this season, had already proved a great tonic if things had gone sour for Spurs. Now Orient's frustration over important league points squandered was relieved by a magnificent European result for Spurs. It worked both ways.

On Saturday lunchtime, I received a couple of texts almost simultaneously. Checking my phone, they were from Jamie and Murph. An Orient newsflash perhaps? Jamie's text was brief and unclear:

'Adam v Cads: Adam made the final cut.'

The cut? What was he on about? I opened Murph's message:

'They picked you over Cads. You did well mate, looked quality. A right geeeeza!'

Suddenly it dawned on me. 'Take It Like A Fan' had chosen my £100 performance over Cadman's £50 effort. They must have cut out the Peter Reid cock-up somehow. I'd got my fifteen minutes of fame, or two or three anyway. What the 'geeeeza' bit referred to, I didn't know.

Then it occurred to me that hundreds of thousands of people would see me completely bottle the double-or-quits question. Hopefully the programme's editors didn't make a big issue of it. Winning £100 was still a decent effort for doing pretty much nothing. There was no shame in being prudent. Hopefully someone had recorded it, or I'd never see it myself on TV!

Orient were back in action in the FA Cup first round at Dagenham and Redbridge. Again they threw away an advantage, going one up through another Alex Revell goal, only to be pegged back almost immediately. The tie went to a replay, but we would miss that fixture at Brisbane Road in favour of saving our cash for a more salubrious venue. Goodbye Leyton, hello Lisbon!

The two-and-a-half hour flight from Luton to Portugal's capital city was as effortless and stress-free as you could hope for with a budget airline. Murph and I arrived at the airport on a drizzly Friday morning and met Luke and Worz, two friends from university and travelling days, at a cafe inside the terminal.

Jamie, in his usual care-free way, maximised his time in bed with his Swedish companion and rocked up to the departure lounge just forty minutes before we were due to take off. It being November, or Movember as he called it, Jamie had taken on the challenge of growing a moustache for charity. He appeared sporting ridiculous-looking whiskers as we sat eating breakfast in a cafe. With much pointing and roars of amusement from us at the table, Jamie grinned sheepishly and took a seat.

'You look like some kind of sexual predator,' Luke managed to force out through a mouthful of baguette.

'You'll never get through passport control looking like that,' I said seriously, while the others cackled with derision. Jamie smiled begrudgingly and patiently, no doubt having had the same treatment for the last week or so from his housemate and work colleagues.

The trip had got off to a hilarious start. Once we'd landed and dumped our luggage, we took a wander through Lisbon's hilly streets and back alleys to find somewhere to eat and drink the afternoon away.

Lisbon, situated on the Poruguese coast, is one of the oldest cities in the world. It has survived earthquakes and invasions and has a wise and robust but laid-back character. Its cobbled streets wound upwards away from the sea in a maze of buildings, shops and bars.

Yet this particular city was not our destination because of its tourist sites, but because of its biggest football club. Having already taken in the San Siro in Milan and Borussia Dortmund's Westfalen Stadium, and with a trip to Barcelona's Camp Nou next year for Murph's stag do also on the cards, we thought a quick weekend sojourn to Lisbon in November would be perfect for our next stop on the football-inspired lads weekend tour. The club we came to see, Benfica, reached a high point in their history when they lifted the European Cup back in 1961 and 1962, beating the Tottenham double-winners in the 1962 semi-final.

Other than watching the football on Sunday evening, we had no plans to partake in cultural activities. Our weekend consisted of lengthy drinking sessions followed by mornings recovering and recuperating. The liveliest area of the city was the neighbourhood known as Bairro Alto, quite literally the Higher District. It is a labyrinth of alleys, home to numerous bars and small clubs whose revellers spill out into the streets and party the night away into the early hours.

The first night we enjoyed far too many liquid refreshments. By 5am we lost Jamie and Murph and were stumbling from venue to venue in blind abandon. So blind that I mistook a brass statue of a musician for a real person and spent a few minutes peering suspiciously at it before venturing a hand to stroke its cold cheek, checking whether my inanimate new friend was for real.

Saturday morning was a struggle, but after a bit of fresh air we felt human enough to find a bar to watch Spurs take on Blackburn. Spurs had never failed to win when I was on the European tour, even managing an incredible 9-1 win against Wigan while I was in Milan. This time was no different and they rolled Blackburn over 4-2, missing a penalty in the process. Orient had an even better time of it, winning 3-0 away at Bristol Rovers, the O's first away win since January 2009. With two wins in the bag and a clearing hangover, a mixture of sickness and fatigue hit me like a train. Realising it had taken me a full hour to get halfway through a pint of lager, I decided enough was enough and returned to the hotel while the others partied on.

Murph rose the next day, as he always seemed to do, at exactly 10 o'clock. We decided that with the others comatose for at least another couple of hours since the last revellers got back after dawn, we should make the most of the day before the Benfica match kicked off. We headed over the water to where the huge Cristo Rei statue stands sentinel over the city. The 28-metre tall statue of Jesus Christ, similar to the one in Rio de Janeiro, stands with arms outstretched atop an 82-metre high monument. Visitors with a head for heights get an incredible panoramic view across the water to the heart of the city, and it captures beautifully the city's rolling topography.

Once everybody was up and mobile, we walked to the nearest Metro station and joined the throng of red-and-white scarves and banners making their way along the Blue Line to the Estadio da Luz. As we approached the stadium, surrounded by hordes of chattering Portuguese fans, we stopped at one of the many stalls selling scarves, hats and other fan paraphernalia.

'Should have remembered what colours Benfica wear,' Murph said as he studied the scarves hanging at the back of the stall. 'Red and white. I could have worn my Orient scarf and saved myself a few quid.'

'You've got to get a scarf mate,' I said. 'It's a souvenir of your visit to Lisbon. You've got to take something away with you other than an empty wallet and a damaged liver.'

Purchases made, and instantly regretted when we realised the scarves were cut to a length that barely reached round our necks, we followed the crowds towards the illuminated bowl that stood out like a beacon amidst the gloom.

We had no trouble getting tickets and only parted with €22 for the privilege, the same price as a ticket at Brisbane Road. We set off round the perimeter of the stadium to find our gate, stopping briefly to get a picture with a bronze statue of Benfica's most famous son, Eusebio.

Built for the 2004 European Championships, the stadium holds over 65,000 spectators. Much like Arsenal's Emirates Stadium, not surprising considering they were both designed by the same architect, the Estadio da Luz has three tiered rings of seats that circle the pitch. We were sat in the lower tier behind the goal. Looking around, it seemed a family occasion. Having located the seats we attempted to purchase some refreshments only to find out that the only beer on offer was non-alcoholic. Whether or not this was a regular occurrence or because it was a Sunday or a family night, it seemed strange since the league itself is sponsored by Portugal's most popular beer, Sagres. Considering our alcohol consumption during the last few days, it was perhaps a blessing that we had no choice but to abstain. We retook our seats to enjoy the entertainment.

An eagle handler entered the field before kick-off and released an enormous brown bird of prey, the symbol of the club, into the air. The crowd cheered and camera bulbs flashed as the eagle soared majestically over the pitch, making several circuits before coming to land back on its perch.

'Maybe we should tell Orient about this,' I said to the others as we tracked the bird's flight path, 'it could be a new tradition to get the crowd going.'

'Knowing our luck the bloody thing would fly off to Upton Park,' Murph said sardonically.

'Yeah, or plough head first into the East Stand to snatch a hot dog,' Jamie added.

The opposition, Naval 1º de Maio, were not much of a team. They were rock bottom of the Portuguese Primeira Liga while Benfica were flying high in second place behind an unbeaten Porto. Benfica, with Argentinean duo Pablo Aimar and Javier Saviola pulling the strings and

Brazilian David Luiz's composed presence in the back four, took their hapless opponents apart. It was another Argentinean, Nicolás Gaitán, who stole the show with a brace of goals, including one spectacular strike from 30 yards. Veteran striker Nuno Gomes rounded off the scoring in a 4-0 victory. We had an enjoyable game, although the rest of the crowd were somewhat subdued and it was a young girl just in front of us, no older than seven years old, who made the most noise.

The trip was a welcome but far from relaxing break and it highlighted again, as our other trips abroad to watch football had done, how far top-flight English football had slipped away from the average supporter. Benfica, Dortmund and Milan are among the best-supported clubs in their respective leagues, and on each occasion we had been able to get tickets easily and cheaply. In contrast, value for money has undoubtedly been taken away from much of the top flight in England. Any attempt to attend one of the biggest clubs in the Premier League on a whim would leave you sorely disappointed or hugely out of pocket.

Yet it is hard to judge the merits of an entire country's football on a one-off game. Portugal suffers a greater amount of predictability than the Premier League. Only two teams besides the big three of Porto, Benfica and Sporting Lisbon have won the championship in the past 75 years and the Portuguese league is blighted by low attendances outside the matches played between the elite clubs. It's always easy to see the positives in something you are completely unfamiliar with when you are focused on the flaws of something you know so well. I wondered how fans of Naval 1° de Maio felt about their lot in life.

Normality returned back in rainy Blighty. I was back to the uncertainty of my job and the equally uncertain fortunes of Orient, of whom I had seen little since the Rochdale game at the end of October. Not wanting to stretch the ever-enduring patience of Stacey, who would most probably have done something unspeakable to my genitals had I told her I was off to Brisbane Road the first night back after a four-day trip to Portugal, I decided not to go to the FA Cup replay against Dagenham and Redbridge. It was the first home fixture I had missed, and judging by the score, it was a bit of a classic.

Orient were two goals to the good at half-time, but in character with their recent form, they allowed the visitors to get it back to 2-2 with two goals in two minutes. A goal from Scott McGleish settled matters in Orient's favour with fifteen minutes to go. The second round draw had already been made, so victorious Orient were rewarded with an away trip to non-league Droylsden, near Manchester. Given the lowly nature of the opposition, the romance of the cup and Orient's inconsistent league form, the TV schedulers anticipated a bit of giant killing and announced it would be shown live. Having never watched Orient on the box, it would be an interesting experience being an armchair O for the day.

Saturday 20th November 2010
Orient v Bournemouth

Three weeks had passed since our last outing to Brisbane Road. I was getting withdrawal symptoms, so it was comforting to know I'd be back in the Tommy Johnston Stand again.

In a case of terrible timing, I had been summoned to Leigh-on-Sea, where my sister Karen and brother-in-law Rob live, for a family photo during the morning. The same day happened to be the first Arsenal-Spurs fixture of the season, and with the match kicking off at 12:45 and the trip back from Essex to Leyton taking at least an hour, I was likely to miss all of the first half and some of the second too.

I boarded the train to London just as the game kicked off. I avoided the score at all costs, not wanting to jinx anything by having the temerity to check. Changing at West Ham and Stratford and on to Leyton, I arrived at a packed Supporters Club with only twenty minutes of the game left. Almost unable to look, I glanced up at the score in the top left of the screen. 2-2. Looked like I'd missed another great match.

The game swung from end-to-end. The crowd gathered inside the Supporters Club was clearly defined into groups supporting Spurs, groups rooting for Arsenal and those who were happy to remain neutral. I watched nervously. With five minutes to go, the tension got to me. I stepped outside to try and pretend that the game wasn't going on, but ruined that plan by peering back through the front window to get a glimpse of the screen.

As I looked on, van der Vaart swung the ball into the Arsenal box from a free kick wide on the right touchline. White and red shirts jostled to meet the approaching ball, but Tottenham defender Younes Kaboul leapt highest and flicked the ball low into the corner into the net.

The inside of the Supporters Club erupted in cheers. Clearly I wasn't the only Spurs supporter who called Orient their second home. I paced up and down outside the club, gulping at my pint with anxious haste before deciding I couldn't hack the last few minutes. I downed the remainder of my drink and entered the ground.

Alone in my seat, phone in hand, I fidgeted. Guessing that the full-time whistle must have blown given the sudden influx of supporters around me, I opened up the phone and waited for the score to load. They'd done it! I sat back in my seat with a big smile on my face, resting my feet on the chair back in front of me, waiting for the boys to arrive.

They didn't turn up until just after kick-off. Murph looked glum, and was accompanied by Pompey-supporting Phil, who had taken Chas' ticket while he continued to convalesce from his back operation. As they approached, Bournemouth scored. If it was possible, Gooner Murph looked even more dejected as he took his seat.

'Commiserations mate,' I offered, not wanting to rub his nose in it. Too much.

'Yeah, well... it's the way it goes,' he said simply. 'Great timing here as well. Haven't even sat down yet and we're losing.'

Having become far too familiar with Murph and Chas mocking me over the years for Spurs' failings, Arsenal's procession of trophies and the abysmal head-to-head record between the teams, I was amazed at my reserve. Inside, I was pointing, laughing, sticking up two fingers and singing 'glory, glory Tottenham Hotspur!' but something was preventing me from externalising this. Perhaps time and continual disappointment had worn me down, or maybe our kinship over Orient had diluted the rivalry between us.

Jamie arrived a few minutes later, looking even worse than Murph.

'Didn't get to bed until eight this morning,' he said as he sat down. 'What's the score?'

'Bournemouth are one-up,' I answered.

'Already? Bollocks!' he sighed.

In spite of being a goal down, it was Orient who were pressing and playing better football. Bournemouth were flying high in the league, but the O's were knocking it about with such confidence and style it was hard to tell who was above who in the table.

The afternoon was bitterly cold so we headed for the warmth of the bar at half-time for a quick pint and to defrost our frozen feet. As we made our way back to our places for the second half, Bournemouth scored again.

'Oh, for fuck's sake!' Murph groaned in exasperation. 'Is this day going to get any worse?'

The second goal seemed to kill Orient's spirit and they began to misplace passes that they pinged around with ease in the first half. The performance deteriorated, and with ten minutes to go Murph had enough.

'This isn't my day,' he shivered. 'I'm freezing cold and we're getting dicked on. Let's just go and have a pint.'

We sat in one of the booths in the bar beneath the Tommy Johnston Stand and began moaning about the performance, but then suddenly heard a muffled cheer and banging.

The announcer read out the name of Jonathan Téhoué, fresh from the substitute bench, as the Orient goal scorer. We looked up at the TV screen on the wall a moment later to see that it read Orient 1, Bournemouth 3.

'Did they score again?' Phil said in surprise. 'I didn't hear anything.'

None of us had heard a sound, but a couple of minutes later there was another loud cheer and even more banging.

'Must be 3-2 now then,' I said as we turned around to the TV screen again to see the confirmation. We jumped from our seats in surprise at what we saw.

Leyton Orient 2, Bournemouth 2. Téhoué (90+2).

'They pulled it back?' Murph yelled, looking astonished. 'But it said 3-1 a second ago?'

'They must have ballsed up the screen or something,' Jamie said, looking equally as dumbfounded as the rest of us.

The full-time result flashed up a moment later. Sure enough, the game had ended 2-2.

Football is a funny old game as the old adage goes, and we learned a thoroughly important lesson. Never, no matter how bleak the situation is, leave a football match early. You have no idea what might happen. Spurs had come from two goals down at the Emirates Stadium, now Orient had pulled back a draw from the same situation. It's not over until it's over, even in injury time when opposition substitutes are coming on with silly grins on their faces as if the points are already in the bag. Football has the ability to ruin an afternoon, but it can also surprise and delight when the odds are stacked against you.

A few days later, Orient's mini-revival continued with another draw away at Peterborough United. The O's were twice a goal behind, but for the second time in three days a late strike, this time from Jimmy Smith, grabbed a point for the visitors. There was even time for Orient's stand-in goalkeeper Jason Brown, on loan from Blackburn Rovers, to save a penalty with almost the last touch of the game. The draw moved the O's up to nineteenth in the table.

The second round of the FA Cup was played over the following weekend, with Orient's televised game against Droylsden scheduled for a Monday night slot on ESPN. The third round draw was made before the match, on Sunday evening. The O's were ball number 52 in the draw, and I also had my eye on Spurs at number 39. What if they got drawn together? What would I do? It went all the way down to the last four balls, when Spurs and Orient remained in the pot with Norwich and Charlton. It was not to be, the O's were drawn away at Championship side Norwich City, assuming that they could avoid the banana skin in the north-west.

A slip-up against Droylsden was a real possibility because the pitch was a veritable ice rink. The grass at the Butcher's Arms Ground was surrounded on all sides by mounds of snow that had been pushed from the pitch, but the perimeter of the playing surface was frozen solid and the middle was boggy and wet. The ground was so small and the cameras so close to the crowd that almost every utterance could be heard. There must have been a good number of travelling supporters as recognisably cockney voices could be heard swearing and laughing on the sidelines.

After 25 minutes of scrappy football and much sliding around, Droylsden took a shock but deserved lead after a free kick was headed home at close range. Orient's typically poor set piece defending was haunting them again. They improved in the second half, and the superior fitness of professional sportsmen began to tell as the visitors pressed for an equaliser to prevent the very real possibility of an embarrassing exit to part-timers. Thankfully, Scott McGleish struck with fifteen minutes to go to. The Os' blushes were spared, but a winner never materialised and Droylsden held on to claim a creditable draw to force a replay.

As Orient slid around the pitch and slogged to a hard-fought draw against lowly opposition on a wintry night in

Manchester in an archetypal English cup tie, on another TV channel, European giants Real Madrid faced rivals Barcelona in their first meeting of the season. In what was reportedly one of the finest footballing displays ever, the Catalans stormed to a 5-0 win.

I texted Murph to ask him which game he'd elected to watch. His message back had me nodding in agreement. 'O's game mate. What a chore. Did you see the Barca result? We must be insane.'

Yes, we were mad, though not as insane as those Orient fans who braved the sub-zero temperatures to make the journey to Droylsden. That was real dedication.

```
16.Plymouth Argyle.....P18|W6 |D4 |L8 |F23|A29|22pts
17.Bristol Rovers......P18|W5 |D7 |L6 |F21|A28|22pts
18.Tranmere Rovers.....P18|W6 |D4 |L8 |F19|A26|22pts
19.Leyton Orient.......P18|W5 |D6 |L7 |F25|A25|21pts
20.Swindon Town........P18|W5 |D6 |L7 |F28|A32|21pts
21.Notts County........P17|W6 |D1 |L10|F21|A28|19pts
22.Dagenham&Redbridge..P18|W3 |D6 |L9 |F19|A32|15pts
```

December 2010

Spurs ended November with a 2-1 triumph over Liverpool following yet another late goal – perhaps both Spurs and Orient had thrown off the shackles and would never throw away a lead again? Not likely. Anyway, Spurs had beaten Liverpool, Arsenal and Inter, while Orient had made some progress too. Two draws snatched from the very brink of defeat was an enormous step in the right direction. A packed schedule lay ahead.

Before that, the world was waiting for FIFA President Sepp Blatter to announce which countries were successful in their bids to host the World Cup in 2018 and 2022. England, with figurehead David Beckham, mounted a strong campaign to host the 2018 competition and had overcome some significant hurdles: the resignation of bid chairman Lord Triesman, a change in government and the wrath of FIFA Vice-President Jack Warner over allegations of corruption.

England could have hosted the tournament immediately in already-existing stadia, yet the predictions from commentators were not hopeful. But with Beckham, Prime Minister David Cameron and royal heir Prince William politicking in Switzerland until the last minute, there was still an outside chance England could get the required votes to host the World Cup for the first time since 1966. With fond memories of the England-based European Championships in 1996, I was excited to think that the greatest competition in world sport could come to our shores.

On the day of the draw itself I was surprisingly nervous, particularly as England's chances were slim to none. Like the build up to a big game of football, the anticipation of a positive result and what it would mean had got my imagination running wild. I would be sat in a new Tottenham ground on a balmy June night eight years in the future, watching England trash Germany. Perhaps I'd have a young son looking on excitedly beside me, being inspired to begin a football career that would take him into the England team in 2028…

Snapping out of my daydream, it was time for the announcement. I scrambled around trying to plug my headphones in to follow the result live on the internet. Early rumours were not good. Gary Lineker, who had played an important role as an ambassador in the England bid, passed on some news he had been given. It was still unconfirmed, but England's bid, with all the stadia, history and commercial potential, had failed to get through the first round of voting. No-one was confident.

Two of FIFA's executive committee members were suspended over charges of alleged corruption, so the magic number that bidding nations needed to reach was twelve from the remaining 22 members.

Sepp Blatter, smiling benignly, approached the podium. After a lengthy preamble, the aged FIFA president pulled a large square envelope open, paused briefly, and announced Russia would host the World Cup in 2018.

The cheers and applause from the Russian delegation vanished as I threw the headphones off in disgust and broke the news to my colleagues. Before picking the headphones back up to hear the outcome of the 2022 vote, I turned to my boss and said, 'if Qatar get 2022, you know this has been one big fix!'

A short time later, once the stage had cleared of celebrating oligarchs, Blatter opened a second envelope. Tugging on the piece of paper within, he revealed that the tiny nation of Qatar had indeed won the 2022 vote ahead of the USA, South Korea, Japan and Australia. In pulling out that small scrap of paper, Blatter metaphorically pulled the chain on my interest in international football.

Russia's choice had a whiff of the suspicious about it owing to the influence of the country's oil barons like Roman Abramovich, but it made some footballing sense. At least they played football and produced some good footballers. Qatar's appointment stunk to high heaven. The national team was ranked around 100 in the world.

That a country the size of a postage stamp with a less impressive sporting heritage than the Isle of Wight could be given the right to host the World Cup is a disgrace. It seemed like the rich had paid off the greedy. It was no longer about the fans, the memories or the glory. It came down to the highest bidder, not the most suitable. All the safety records, stadia, transport infrastructure and marketability in the world would not change that.

England received just two votes, and one of those was from English executive committee member Geoff Thompson. Eighteen months and an £18 million campaign and England only managed to persuade one other committee member to vote for them.

FIFA's rotation policy quite rightly takes the World Cup tournament to all corners of the globe, so another European-hosted World Cup would not be available until 2030. I would be approaching 50 years old before Britain had the chance to host a World Cup again, and that thought made me forlorn.

Did it really matter? A sense of apathy has surrounded the national team since the 2007 European Championship qualifying debacle. Many diehard fans who wouldn't dream of missing a club fixture can't be bothered to tune in to international friendlies. Of those that do, it is with a feeling of reluctant duty more than anything else. Watching England has taken on the characteristics of a visit to the dentist, you don't want to do it, but somehow you feel it's something you have to.

The truth of the matter is that they just haven't been good enough when it matters. Call it a lack of big game mentality, or blame underfunded grassroots football or antiquated coaching methods if you like, but whenever the pressure is on, they freeze and let the country down. England's superstars haven't helped themselves – they've been caught out shagging around, missing drugs tests and fighting in nightclubs. Inevitably, the press turn on them and lead the public in the consensus of opinion that the England team is over-hyped and over-paid.

Had England's bid been successful, a wave of positivity and pride similar to that which washed over the country in 1996 might have returned and sparked a revival in passion towards the national team. Now we will never find out, at least not for another couple of decades in any case. Before that the only chance of such a revival will come if England's players bring home a trophy, and that is as likely as Orient lifting the FA Cup.

League One football was a welcome and honest refuge from the World Cup shenanigans, but there was little on offer. Cold weather had the whole of Britain in an icy grip and clubs up and down the country were forced to postpone matches. 27 games in the football league fell victim to the weather, and Orient's clash with Carlisle was one of them.

Orient managed to thaw out the Brisbane Road pitch for the replay against Droylsden a few days later. It was another freezing cold night and after watching the dull first match on ESPN a week or so earlier, none of us fancied shelling out on tickets for what was likely to be a poor game in near arctic conditions.

That decision looked to have been vindicated as I checked the score midway through the second half. The non-league side were 2-0 up and Orient's centre-back Terrell Forbes had been sent off. With a sigh I closed the screen and set the computer on the floor, the plans for a Norwich away day fading into the cold December night.

Some time later, to confirm my assumption that Droylsden were by now halfway back up the M1 celebrating their giant-killing on the team coach, I opened the laptop back up. My jaw dropped. Orient had taken the game to extra time in the last minute, both teams finished with nine men, Scott McGleish and Jonathan Téhoué scored hat-tricks and the O's emphatically knocked out the weary and shell-shocked part-timers 8-2, scoring six goals in the extra half hour.

Shaking my head in utter disbelief, I fired off a quick text to the others. 'Looks like we missed game of the season! Whose great idea was it not to go?'

The same night, Spurs played out a thrilling 3-3 draw in Holland against FC Twente to guarantee they topped their Champions League group and qualified for the last 16. Given the inauspicious start they made in the competition back in early August, topping the group was something no Spurs fan predicted. The way they approached their Champions League adventure had won plaudits from all over. They took to games with such attacking abandon that teams had been overawed before they had a chance to get started. The only club to have scored more times than Spurs in the group stages was Barcelona.

The following week, a full league schedule was back. Orient travelled to Tranmere, who like us, were hovering just above the relegation zone. Both sides needed a win, so it was likely to be a close, tense affair. I spent another Saturday afternoon glued to *Soccer Saturday* and was texting back and forth as Orient took a healthy 2-0 lead into the half-time break with goals from Dawson and McGleish. Then they conceded a sloppy goal from a set piece and were left with half an hour to hold on. Murph and I continued our game of text tennis, both as nervous as the other, as the minutes ticked down. At last the vidiprinter put us out of our misery, flashing up the final score from Prenton Park. Orient had seen the game through and had increased their unbeaten run to eight in all competitions. Slowly but surely, we were climbing the table.

Christmas party season was in full swing, and despite the doom and gloom of potential unemployment still hanging over me like a Dickensian ghost of Christmases yet-to-come, the frivolity and merriment continued unabated. Although the weather had been a thorn in the side of groundsmen for the past few weeks, it was providing a glorious wintry backdrop for the Christmas period. Plymouth Argyle were due at Brisbane Road on the final weekend before Christmas, and as we were unlikely to see each other until just before New Year at the earliest, we planned to use the game as a springboard for our own festive celebrations. Murph had procured seven extra tickets to the weekend's game and ordered Santa suits from an online shop. Eleven jolly, bearded and half-cut Saint Nicks dressed head-to-toe in Orient red seemed like a perfect way to get in the Christmas spirit, and I was looking forward to the weekend immensely.

The wintery conditions returned, and by Thursday the streets of London were an inch deep in snow. The two-and-a-half mile walk to work through slush and ice was a treacherous affair, so I knew the Brisbane Road pitch would be in bad shape. Plymouth had a 500-mile round trip from Devon to the capital and wouldn't want to make the journey if there was a chance the match would be called off. The signs were ominous. Sure enough, by midday on Friday the Orient website bore the bad news. For the second time in a month, our trip to Brisbane Road was called off. Our Santa suits were unopened and unused. We'd have looked a bit foolish wearing them for the rearranged date in April.

Stacey and I spent Christmas Day with my family at my sister's in Leigh-on-Sea. I enjoyed the company of both Mum and Dad for the first time in about seventeen years – they divorced years ago but remain friends. It was a wonderfully relaxed afternoon. My young niece and nephew were playing excitedly with their new toys, which gave me an excuse to do the same and indulge my inner child. Stace will say that's an urge I rarely suppress.

My sister also revealed that she had recorded my TV debut. With my family watching on, I hit play. There I was peering back through the screen on 'Take It Like A Fan', making a passable attempt at looking like an East End hard nut.

'This is Adam,' the voice over said, 'and he's a right geeeeza!' My family rolled about with laughter as my face went crimson in embarrassment.

'You look good on screen,' Stace said defensively, trying to see the bright side.

Despite the cockney wide boy image they had painted me with, it was a bit of a thrill. The questions came and went, and it surprised me that I'd forgotten so many that they asked. Try as I might, I couldn't spot the cleanly-edited join where the question about Thailand's manager was surreptitiously removed.

'I think that went alright,' I said as the questions drew to a close. 'Didn't come out of it looking a total wally at least.'

I spoke too soon. As I declined the option to attempt the double-or-quits question, an image flashed up on screen. It was gone in the blink of an eye, but I knew what it meant. For no more than two or three frames, the clever editing team had put an image of a milk bottle in place of my head, drawing full attention to the fact I had bottled the question. I hoped they'd let me get away with it. I was wrong.

Grimacing and shaking my head, I turned off the recording; my brother-in-law and dad howling with derisive laughter behind me.

Orient's Boxing Day home fixture against MK Dons was called off, the third league match in a row. That was good news because I had already agreed with Stace that we would visit her dad in St Albans that day. I could keep my unblemished home league attendance record intact when the game was rearranged for some time in the New Year.

It did mean that I had failed to see a single Orient game throughout the whole of December, and the team itself only played two. So many games were called off that the proposal for a winter break once again reared its head. The national team's poor showing in international tournaments is often put down to player fatigue, and almost all of northern Europe's major leagues take a break over the Christmas and New Year period.

Yet the traditional Christmas fixtures are popular among fans and many do not want to lose them. While a break may do the players good in the short term, the fixture lists are already full. Two or three weeks off would just mean cramming in more games at a later stage in the season. Only reducing the amount of teams in the league would seem to solve that quandary.

Orient's future fixtures were starting to mount up, in common with other clubs. With cup finals and play-offs at the end of May, it would be a tight fit to slot the postponed matches into the months ahead.

Tottenham were in with a shout for the league at the halfway stage, having gone unbeaten in December, and were only five points from top spot. They were also in the last sixteen of the Champions League. I was watching events unfold from a distance, behind a screen and in newspaper columns.

Yet glory can come in many forms. I didn't expect Orient to win the FA Cup any more than I thought Spurs would win the Champions League. But Orient were marching up the table, playing some excellent football and were into the FA Cup third round. More importantly, I was there to see it all with my own eyes, accompanied by friends who were sharing the experience with me. We had match day rituals, knew the regular fans and were starting to be recognised and acknowledged in return. As a new year approached, we felt we belonged.

```
14.Carlisle United.....P19|W7 |D6 |L6 |F26|A20|27pts
15.Plymouth Argyle.....P20|W7 |D5 |L8 |F26|A30|26pts
16.Swindon Town........P20|W6 |D7 |L7 |F31|A34|25pts
17.Leyton Orient.......P19|W6 |D6 |L7 |F27|A26|24pts
18.Notts County........P19|W7 |D2 |L10|F24|A29|23pts
19.Rochdale............P19|W5 |D7 |L7 |F27|A26|22pts
20.Tranmere Rovers.....P19|W6 |D4 |L9 |F20|A28|22pts
```

January 2011

Stace and I welcomed in the New Year without much fuss. With offers of parties from friends on both sides, we decided the diplomatic thing to do was to politely decline everybody and enjoy our own company instead. New Year's Eve is usually a bit of a let down anyway. You pay twice the money to go to a doubly-busy venue and wait twice as long to get a drink; the only differentiating feature from any other night of the year comes in the ten seconds to midnight when you count backwards until the clock strikes twelve. I could do without the expense, and with redundancy still a distinct possibility, I needed to keep a watchful eye on my outgoings.

I may have avoided the let down of New Year's Eve, but I couldn't escape the let down of New Year's Day.

Orient's unbeaten streak ended abruptly at the hands of a rampant Brighton. There must have been a few hangovers in the O's dressing room as the runaway leaders of League One smashed five unanswered goals past their hapless opponents. Although Orient had made gradual improvements in their form and results, the thrashing was a timely reminder that there was still a lot of work to be done.

<u>Monday 3rd January 2011</u>
<u>Orient v Colchester United</u>

I shrugged off the 5-0 defeat easily, eager as I was to return and see live football for the first time in over a month. The icy weather had departed and although winter's chill still hung in the air, there was no chance that this game would be called off.

Whilst rummaging around in the loft for the Christmas decorations, I had rediscovered my old Orient scarf that I bought more than ten years before on one of my first ever visits to Brisbane Road. With the scarf slung loosely around my neck, I marched proudly to Jamie's flat to pick up his ticket. He had just arrived back from another trip to Ireland and I was meeting the others at the ground well before kick-off to buy our tickets for the Norwich FA Cup tie. Jamie was in no fit state for an early start, opening the door in his dressing gown, bleary eyed and yawning. He thrust the ticket into my waiting hand and muttered 'I'll see you down there' as he closed the door.

I walked down through Weavers Fields to Bethnal Green station and only had a minute to wait for my train to rattle in. I climbed aboard as the doors slid open and my heart sank immediately. A large bunch of young Colchester fans were occupying seats on both sides of the carriage. The cheers and laughter as they spotted my scarf made me cringe. Why did I pick this day to break out my old scarf and then choose this bloody carriage to get on? The taunting chants began. There was nothing offensive, so I stood smiling wryly and trying not to make too much eye contact.

'Ask 'im, he'll know,' I heard one of the U's supporters say, and looking up, I saw he was pointing at me.

''Scuse me mate,' the ringleader said, 'what stop do we 'ave to get off for the Coach n 'orses? Is it Leyton or Leytonstone?'

The Coach and Horses pub on Leyton High Road was the designated venue for away supporters and was a just a short walk from the ground. Toying with the idea of telling them to get off at the wrong station, my Good Samaritan instinct kicked in and I dutifully informed them that Leyton was the station they required. They thanked me and restarted their chorus of Colchester United songs.

'We hate Southend and we hate Southend, we hate Southend and we hate Southend, we hate Southend and we hate Southend, we are the Southend haters!'

They clapped and banged on the windows as fellow passengers stirred uncomfortably in their seats and looked furtively at the Colchester fans as if they were a crowd of marauding Vikings. I continued my smiling ambivalence. I wondered what they'd say if I mentioned that I was born in the town they purported to hate so much?

The journey seemed to last for ever. We pulled into Mile End station and some relieved-looking passengers scuttled off and vanished up the stairs.

'Ooo are ya, ooo are ya, ooo are ya?'

This one was directed at me, so I played up to them and kissed my scarf, waggling a tasselled end, emblazoned with the Orient crest, in their direction. That got a bit of a laugh.

The tube approached Stratford and a girl in her early twenties got meekly to her feet and headed for the doors.

'Does she take it up the arse? Does she take it up the arse?'

The mortified girl folded her arms tightly across her chest as if bracing herself for a nasty collision and exited the carriage, head bowed. Feeling embarrassed for the poor girl, I shook my head. The other passengers squirmed in their seats, anxious to get off the train as soon as they could. What makes football fans lose all sense of social morality when they get in a group?

The singing and chanting continued as we approached Leyton station and it was with relief that I exited the train and climbed the stairs to where Murph and Chas were waiting for me. The Colchester fans filed past me outside the station and a few smiled and thanked me again for the help. They weren't bad lads, just boisterous and excited for the day's game. It can be intimidating to others, as had been shown by the reactions of the other passengers on the tube, but I knew that these lads were harmless enough.

'Oh my days,' I said to the others as we trooped off down the road. 'That felt like the longest tube ride ever!'

I explained what I'd just gone through as we walked down towards the ground. It was good to see Chas again. Having spent six weeks recovering from surgery, this was his first game at Brisbane Road since the win over Hartlepool in the middle of October. Fortunately for him the snow and ice had postponed all but two of the games he would otherwise have missed.

After picking up our Norwich tickets, we whiled away the time until kick-off in the Supporters Club discussing the big issues in the country as we saw them: the use of Twitter by footballers, the over-the-top sensitivity of Liverpool fans and whether Ian Holloway was a potential England manager.

Jamie arrived with half an hour to go until kick-off. He filled us in on his antics over the Christmas period, which included waking up stark naked in his mate's sister's bed early on Christmas morning and having to sneak out of the front door to avoid being seen. He was abstaining from alcohol after a heavy couple of weeks.

With the game about to start we made our way to the Tommy Johnston Stand and took up the cry of 'Orieeeeent, Orieeeeeeent!' that was already echoing around the ground.

'Aaaah, it's good to be back,' Chas declared, stretching his arms out wide and scanning the pitch appreciatively.

He was right. It was good to be back.

Orient started the game brightly and looked nothing like a team who had just come off the back of a 5-0 thumping. Yet despite the confident start, the game soon turned scrappy and Orient returned to their sloppy ways.

Thankfully, Colchester were looking equally wasteful in possession and just before half-time Orient managed to take one of the few chances that came their way. Dean Cox curled in a dangerous cross, and from twelve yards out midfielder Jimmy Smith ghosted into the box, looped a header over the U's keeper and into the goal. The home crowd leapt to their feet with joy, and as the clapping and cheering began to subside, I hollered a chant heralding our goalscorer. 'Na na na na na na na na, Jimmy Jimmy Smith, Jimmy Smith, Jiiimmy Jimmy Smith!' I bellowed, to the tune of 'Baby Give it Up' – stealing and reworking the chant Spurs fans use for van der Vaart. I had no idea if it would even be heard but I sang it anyway and to my surprise a thousand or so happy Orient fans took up the song. Sitting down feeling very pleased with myself, the voice of Paul from the seats behind said, 'that was a good one, can't believe we haven't thought of it before!'

Just after half-time, with the warming glow of hot Bovril coursing through our frozen veins, Orient doubled their lead when Alex Revell latched on to a lucky break and fired past the keeper. The crowd were jumping now, going through the full repertoire of Orient songs.

With twenty minutes left and Orient looking comfortable, Colchester launched a hopeful high ball into the Orient penalty area. Jamie Jones, back between the posts after a long injury lay-off, scampered off his line and leapt into the air to claim the ball. To gasps from the crowd, he fumbled the catch and Anthony Wordsworth was on hand for Colchester to turn it in the unguarded net.

A few concerned faces began to shoot knowing glances at each other, as if to say 'here we go again'. But there was no need for panic as young Spurs loanee Paul-Jose M'Poku, on as a substitute once more, struck a beautiful shot into the top corner to take back Orient's two goal advantage.

'Du du duuuu Paul-Jose M'Poku, du du duuuu Paul-Jose M'poku,' we sang. It never ceases to amaze me how quickly football supporters can tailor even the most obscure names into melodious little one-liners.

Another smash-and-grab goal from Colchester was the result of an excellent solo run and finish from forward Ian Henderson, making the score 3-2.

'They can never do things the easy way, this lot!' a middle aged man in front of me said turning to his mate sitting beside him.

What could have been a very nervy ending to the game was settled with less than five minutes to go as Jonathan Téhoué, supersub as usual, ran on to a through ball and poked it past the goalkeeper to wrap things up.

After the final whistle had gone, we made our way to the exit. 'I knew when it was 2-0 we had it in the bag 'cos of the solid defence we've got,' Murph said, his voice laced with sarcasm. A few of the old boys waiting in line overheard and laughed at his gallows humour. They'd seen it all before. Although Orient had won, they would have to tighten up at the back if they wanted to continue climbing the league table.

It was the first time all four of us had been present at Brisbane Road to enjoy an Orient win, four and a half months after we first started going. Whether that said more about our collective commitment or to Orient's poor early season form I wasn't sure. There was no time to salute the landmark day with a couple of celebratory drinks since we were all back to work the next morning. Now we had broken the duck, we would surely have plenty more wins to enjoy together before the end of the season.

The next few days in the office were as tedious and miserable as I expected them to be. No-one seemed remotely enthused by what lay ahead. The outsourcing pilot programme ramped up another level, leaving us with even less to do.

Spurs lost 2-1 away at Everton ending an eleven-game unbeaten streak. With the transfer window back open again, the rumour mill had gone into overdrive. It seemed that David Beckham may join Tottenham on loan from LA Galaxy. The thought of seeing an aging Beckham in a Spurs shirt didn't fill me with too much excitement. Although he is still an excellent professional, what pace he ever had was gone and his role at clubs only ever seemed to be commercially motivated, be it selling shirts or revelling in the international exposure Beckham's presence provides.

Some excitement was provided by Chas. I suggested some time ago that we ask Orient if they'd let us film the players giving Murph and Danielle a wedding message that we would present to the newlyweds on their big day in July. Unbeknownst to me, Chas had made contact with the club and to our delight and surprise they were happy to be involved.

Chas arranged for us to visit the Orient training ground near Ilford on Thursday 27th January. It meant taking a day off work, but that was a small price to pay. It was a testament to the club's commitment to the community and their fans that they were willing to take time out to help us. I wondered how many Premier League clubs would be so welcoming. The supporter-player bond has never been so weak at the top clubs. Players are closeted away from the public after games and rarely interact with their supporters beyond obligatory meet and greets. It would be an interesting experience to see where a League One team trains, how they interact with each other and how they respond to a couple of random blokes coming in to talk to them.

Saturday 8th January 2011
Norwich City v Orient

The road to Wembley took us in the wrong direction on a two-hour trip north to Norwich. The train was due to leave at 10 o'clock from Liverpool Street station. I popped into the supermarket to buy a sandwich for my breakfast and met Murph and Chas in the McDonald's on the corner of the station's upper level. Jamie arrived soon after, sniffling and moaning about a cold. I wasn't surprised he was ill given the temperature and the abuse he had put his body through over Christmas.

On the platform, waiting for the train, I tore open the wrapping on my sandwich. Lifting out one of the halves, I took a huge bite and began to chomp through it, only to hear a click and feel something hard against my cheek.

'Oh bollocks!' I groaned, realising what I'd done.

Reaching a finger into my mouth, I pulled out the object. It was the bridgework and crown of a dental fixture I had fitted about a decade before. I turned it over in my palm, but it was just a mush of enamel, bread and saliva. I examined the gap and jagged stump of a tooth that remained in my mouth where the bridgework had been lifted from. The others looked disgusted as I showed them the offending article and explained what had just happened.

'What a great start to the day that is,' I grumbled as we boarded the train. 'That's gonna cost a bloody fortune to repair.'

The train lurched and snaked out of the station into the light of a cold, grey morning. Spots of rain began to spread across the windows. The train filled up with Orient supporters as we passed through Stratford and Shenfield. Surprisingly, most got on in Colchester. On a good day, that is a 45-minute journey to London.

It highlighted the disparate nature of Orient's fanbase. Many will have grown up around Leyton and moved out to places like Essex and the home counties as they got older, leaving behind a new community heavily populated by immigrants. The collective influx of Asian, Caribbean and eastern Europeans migrants who live there now aren't likely to care too much about unglamorous little Orient on their doorstep and would more than likely adopt clubs like Arsenal, Spurs and Chelsea as their London team.

Orient's support is an aging one. Once they begin to die off, will there be enough of a younger generation remaining to take up the reigns? I was enjoying supporting Orient and was doing my bit to help them this season, but would I continue to do so, or would I abandon them like a used toy?

The Orient message boards were buzzing all week with talk of which pub to meet at. The consensus was the Compleat Angler, beside a bridge on the canal just a short walk from the station. We found a seat in the conservatory, ordered some pints and settled in to watch Arsenal play Leeds in the FA Cup's early kick-off. Slowly but surely, the pub filled up with Orient supporters. Dagenham had been our first official away trip, but now we felt part of the club and this felt more like a proper away day. Everyone was in good spirits and it was good to mix with some unfamiliar faces for a change.

Arsenal managed to scrape a replay with a penalty in the final minute after going a goal down. They played terribly, but Murph and Chas, who usually got excited when watching their team in action, didn't seem remotely bothered.

With kick-off fast approaching and supporters beginning to leave for the ground, I dashed to the loo. Whilst in full stream, a tall, burly O's fan, who had been looking at me curiously and somewhat unnervingly said, 'I fawt I recognised you.'

Unable to reciprocate the recognition, I merely raised my eyebrows and nodded noncommittally. 'You were on that 'Take It Like A Fan' programme weren't ya?' he smiled, washing his hands. 'How much did you win?'

'A hundred pounds,' I said, feeling like a minor celebrity.

'Yeah, that's right, but you bottled the double-or-quits didn't ya?'

I sighed and nodded. He left the toilets without saying anything further. Typical, no one remembers the glory, they only remember the misery.

We joined the small throng of Orient fans heading towards the ground. Carrow Road sits in a retail park opposite a Morrison's supermarket. It holds a little over 27,000 supporters, but by the looks of the crowd it was unlikely to be a full house.

We entered the Jarrold Stand after placing a couple of bets and found our seats. We were sat to the right of the stand near the goal with around 2,000 Orient supporters who had made the trip north. The noise levels were already surpassing those of a Saturday afternoon fixture at Brisbane Road. Like the Daggers game earlier in the season, it made me wonder why it took an away trip to crank up the volume.

Norwich got the game underway and made all the early running while the O's fans continued their cacophonous medley. We even managed to get a few chants going ourselves. With Norwich providing most of the football on the pitch, it was Orient fans providing the atmosphere in the stands. The home support seemed frozen to their seats by the cold weather.

On a rare foray upfield, Orient forced a corner. 'I hope they don't take it short,' I said to the others. 'Short corners never work and it's such a waste of a good position.'

They took it short and I groaned, but before I could do anything else, Dean Cox turned, cut inside and clipped a pin-point cross to Jimmy Smith who was waiting on the six-yard box. Smith connected perfectly with his head and guided the ball into the top corner past the flailing limbs of Declan Rudd in the Norwich goal.

The Orient support went loopy. As I jumped on the spot, punching the air and yelling 'yeeeeeeessssssss' like a South American commentator yells 'gol', Murph shot past me and into a crowd of writhing bodies to my right whooping wildly. Smith span round and ran toward the jubilant crowd pursued by his beaming team mates and slid, arms outstretched and flat on his back, across the damp turf.

After several minutes of baiting the home crowd with shouts of 'who are ya?' which provoked a reaction of the two-fingered variety, both the match and crowd settled back down. Norwich pressed hard for the remainder of the half but our defence, the one Murph joked about only a few days before, was holding firm.

A lady behind us who we recognised from behind the bar in the Supporters Club said her seven-year-old daughter fell asleep on her lap just before we had scored, and the same thing happened the previous week against Colchester. 'My eldest went to the loo on 42 minutes last week and Orient scored then too,' she said to us, 'so I'll make sure she goes again before half-time today, just in case.'

The second superstition failed to have the desired effect and the half-time whistle blew with Orient still one goal to the good. We descended below the stands to warm up a bit and have a pint, and joined in the joyous chanting that had begun in the queue for refreshments. Even Jamie managed to start one off in spite of his sniffles.

The second half was an anxious affair. Orient were penned in for much of it and it took a couple of excellent saves from Jamie Jones and some timely tackles from Terrell Forbes and Ben Chorley to keep the score as it was. Darkness descended over the ground as the game approached its conclusion. Orient barely mustered an effort on goal in the second half, and although Norwich pressed and pressed, it was looking increasingly likely that their efforts were going to remain unrewarded.

As the clock approached 90 minutes, the singing started again, but more nervously this time. The assistant stepped forward and held up the board showing that there would be four added minutes. The faces around me looked fretful. Whistles and shouts begin to rain down on the referee, willing him to blow for full-time. It was an agonising wait.

Norwich had one last attempt which for a moment looked like it was creeping in the bottom corner, but Jones reached across to palm it behind. The subsequent corner was floated in. The ball pinged around the crowded area and fell to a Norwich player at the edge of the box who steadied himself before rifling the ball goalwards. To thankful cheers of relief from the Orient fans, it sailed high and wide over the cross bar.

The final whistle was met with another crescendo of noise. We danced about like madmen and sang ourselves hoarse. The players came over to join the celebrations, Coxy handed his shirt to a young boy in the front row.

We left the ground in full voice. An elderly Norwich fan approached us and congratulated our team on a fine win. It was a nice touch and epitomised the friendly nature of the afternoon. There had been no trouble, no fights or arguments and this old Norwich fan's gracious praise in the face of defeat was a mark of a hospitable and welcoming club. We marched off down the street drunk on victory rather than lager, singing loudly into the Norfolk night.

We celebrated our fine win with a curry and a few more beers. On our way down to the train station we passed a kebab house that was blaring techno music from its warm interior. Looking through the glass frontage we were amused to see Paul, our neighbour in the Tommy Johnston Stand, dancing excitedly on his own to the beat. He paused, saw us looking at him, waved maniacally and went back to busting shapes. By the time we arrived at Liverpool Street at 11pm, Chas had already passed out and the rest of us were yawning and looking exhausted. It had been a long day but the cup run continued. We just had to wait and see who we got in the next round.

The draw took place the following day. Spurs were in the pot after beating Charlton, but this time it was only Orient's ball, number 31, that I had my eye on. Out it came, a fourth round tie away at Swansea. Another potential away trip perhaps? Probably not. It was three-hour schlep across the country and twice as expensive as the Norwich trip. Swansea fans also had a bit of a reputation and I didn't fancy travelling all that way to get a black eye. I could get that in Shoreditch if I tried hard enough.

Later on that evening my mum called to tell me my nan had been taken in to hospital with a chest infection. She had been in and out of hospital so many times over the last five years that it felt like I'd visited her more times at Queen's Hospital than in her own house in Essex. My grandad had maintained their seats at Upton Park all the time she had been unwell, hoping that maybe she would be well enough to go again at some point, but she hadn't been for years.

My mum had gone with him that afternoon to watch West Ham beat Barnsley 2-0 and we chatted about the game for a while. I made loose arrangements to meet her in the week and visit Nanna in the hospital.

The next morning I was yawning loudly in the kitchen, putting the kettle on. As I poured the milk into the cup I heard my phone ring from in the bedroom.

'Who is it Stace?' I shouted, leaving my tea and going back through to the bedroom.

'It's your mum,' she said, looking quizzical and handing me the phone.

'Hello?' I said down the phone. 'Everything alright?' It was 8 o'clock on a Monday morning and I had just spoken to her the night before, so it was an unusual time to call.

'Hi,' she said quietly. After a short pause she stuttered, 'Nanna died last night.' She said the words slowly and in a broken, staccato manner, as if regretting every word as soon as she had said it. She explained to me what had happened and I listened in silence, nodding occasionally. Stace looked at my blank expression and read from it what had happened.

'Is it Nanna?' she mouthed, and I nodded at her grimly.

Hanging up the call, I told Stace what had happened and then walked into the living room to sit on the sofa. I felt numb. She was an elderly lady and had been very ill over the last few years so her death was not altogether unexpected, but I had never experienced this feeling of loss before and I felt unsure of what to do.

Stace came in and sat down, putting an arm around me. I looked past her into the kitchen at the mug of tea I had just made, now alone on the work surface getting cold. All thoughts of breakfast, work and life in general vanished from my mind. I turned to Stace, took one look at her sad eyes, and broke down on her shoulder.

Once I pulled myself together, I called my boss and said I wasn't coming in. Work could go fuck itself for all I cared. I was not remotely in the mood. Instead, we headed over to Battersea Park and wandered peacefully around the pagoda, through the fallen leaves, past joggers, dog walkers and kids riding bikes, as though it were any other day. Years ago, when my nan had been in Lister Hospital, I spent a day in London visiting her and playing in Battersea Park with my sister and cousins. It was the first place that popped in my head that morning when I said I wanted to get out of the house. It seemed fitting somehow. I spoke with my mum again later on and she seemed too dazed to talk clearly about things. She had the formalities of collecting the death certificate and organising the funeral to take care of and her mind was fully occupied.

After the high of Saturday afternoon, I had been brought crashing down to earth. Grief was a new emotion for me to deal with. I spent the day in a daze with Stace having to nudge me out of semi-consciousness after I drifted off into another daydream.

I sat chatting to Stace about Nanna in the evening. If it hadn't been for her kindness in giving up her seat at West Ham, I wouldn't have ever gone to see any kind of football until I was much older. Had that been the case I may never have caught the bug at all.

Sky Sports News was on the TV although the volume had been turned right down. Snippets of news flitted in and out of the screen as life outside my family rolled on as normal. Chas sent a text to say that M'Poku had signed until the end of the season. It was banal news, meaningless really, but it was a comfort in a strange way. Life did go on, as the old cliché goes, but after 86 years it went on without Nanna, who was now at peace.

A week later, the cold weather that seemed to have clutched Britain for months suddenly disappeared and it became much milder, but in doing so brought a deluge of rain. I trudged through it to Brentford's Griffin Park to watch the Bees take on Exeter City in the Southern Division Final of the Johnstone's Paint Trophy. An old mate of mine, Saichy, had got two free tickets to the game courtesy of his friend Matt Taylor who just happened to be the Exeter captain.

We met at Holborn station and took the Piccadilly line all the way to South Ealing. This part of London was completely foreign to me and had it not been for the map on my iPhone, we would probably have got hopelessly lost. We were overheard talking about the game as we walked to the ground by an Exeter fan who accompanied us and showed us the way. He followed the Grecians everywhere, and considering the geographical location of the club, that is some feat. The lengths and expense that fans go to never ceases to amaze me, particularly at this level of the sport. Even more incredible was that Exeter had played Brentford just three days earlier in the league, and this chap had made the same 400-mile round trip then too.

Exeter went through the ignominy of relegation from the football league in 2003, spending the following five seasons as a non-league club. Having bounced back with successive promotions, they now shared League One with Orient. They also boast the unusual status of being the first fan-owned club in the football league. Around 3,000 members of the Exeter City Supporters Trust bought the club, balanced the books and helped push them back up the league ladder. It's a commendable action, and certainly in the lower leagues it's a growing trend. Teams such as Ebbsfleet United, FC United of Manchester and AFC Wimbledon have shown how the model can work. It's certainly a movement I could get behind.

Griffin Park is set back from South Ealing Road among terraced houses and is the only club in the country that has a pub on every corner of the ground. It was a shabby looking stadium, in dire need of a face lift or even just a lick of paint.

We were stood with the away support in a standing section on the Brook Road end. Despite its external appearance, it was a good old-fashioned ground. Stood right against the hoardings behind the goal, we were as close to the action as it is possible to be without being stood on the pitch. Saichy even received a text message from a friend watching the game on Sky to say he had caught a glimpse of us on screen.

The game was a frantic end-to-end affair in spite of the heavy rain that began to fall immediately after kick-off. Exeter's fans were loud and unrelenting in their singing; most songs involved either their love of Exeter or their hatred of Plymouth.

At half-time the away fans were celebrating a 1-0 lead after veteran striker Jamie Cureton found the net. While most of the terrace banter was good natured, it turned sour after Brentford equalised midway through the second half. The travelling support took to abusing the Brentford keeper, who was just yards away from them.

With Exeter pushing for a second goal, they won a corner at our end. As the Brentford players trotted back to take up their positions for the set piece, one Exeter fan screamed towards the Brentford player, 'Forster! You fucking poof, you fucking cock-sucking queer! I hope you die of AIDS you cunt!'

As his comrades laughed raucously at what they clearly believed to be a witty jibe, Saichy and I turned to each other with mouths open in disbelief. A lot of unpleasant things can be heard in the stands at football matches, but there is a line between what can and can't be tolerated. That guy crossed it. A part of me was disappointed in myself for not saying something. I wouldn't accept that in the street or on a bus and had I been in the familiar surroundings of Brisbane Road I would certainly have said something, but instinct told me that confronting a crowd of West Country lads full of cider was unwise. The banter up until then had been good natured and fun and I admired the Exeter fans for their spirit, but that one moment completely changed my opinion of them.

Back in the Premier League, the transfer window rumbled on with Spurs adding Everton's midfield playmaker Steven Pienaar to their ranks. Spurs old-boy Darren Bent abandoned Sunderland, the club that rescued him from misery at White Hart Lane, for Aston Villa, a club that were below Sunderland in the league. Money talks.

Work was as depressing as ever, but I had been thrown a potential lifeline. A few months before, I had applied for a role in the same company in the Product Development team. I fired off a speculative application and then forgot all about it. The morning after I found out my nan passed away, I returned to work to find an email inviting me to an interview. Searching frantically for the job specification to remind me what it was I had applied for, I prepared as thoroughly as I could. On the day of the interview I gave a decent account of myself, this time avoiding constantly talking about football. If I could get this job it would mean more money, better experience, more challenging work and the potential to maybe save some money for a change. I was quietly confident.

Saturday 22nd January 2011
Orient v Sheffield Wednesday

Change was afoot at Orient too. Joss, the Sunderland fan who educated us on the Monkey Hangers of Hartlepool, decided to buy a half-season ticket and would be joining us for the rest of the season. We assured him it was £150 well spent.

There was the potential of massive change for the club as a whole too, but the signs were that it would not be for the better. London had won the right to host the 2012 Olympics back in 2005 and ever since then the issue of what would happen to the Olympic Stadium in Stratford remained unresolved. Orient owner Barry Hearn had expressed an interest in taking the O's to Stratford as the new stadium's tenants and spent three years negotiating with the Olympic Committee. The capacity would be scaled back after the Games from 80,000 to something more manageable, but Lord Coe, chairman of the 2012 Games, insisted on the running track remaining. That killed off Hearn's plans and the idea was forgotten about. West Ham and Spurs were interested too and put forward bids to the Olympic Games Legacy Committee. Now the issue was coming to a head.

The worry for Orient was that Stratford is just one stop down the Central Line. Although it is in West Ham's borough of Newham instead of Orient's Waltham Forest, it is a catchment area for Orient fans. A bigger club like West Ham or Spurs moving into the area would inevitably hoover up casual fans who fancy a bit of Saturday afternoon football. With higher profile matches round the corner, and in West Ham's case a pledge to offer cheap tickets to ensure the stadium was filled, it was a situation that could be terminal to Orient.

The decision on the preferred bidder would be made in a week's time and Hearn had been all over the media championing the cause of little Leyton Orient. In his words, it was 'a case of Tesco moving next to the little sweet shop on the corner', and should West Ham move in it would kill Orient 'stone dead'. A strongly-worded club statement on the hypocrisy and despicable nature of the Olympic Stadium bid meant that the newspapers had at last picked up on the issue. Orient received a fair amount of media coverage as a result.

The Supporters Club was running a petition and fans were being urged to put their name to it to voice their dissatisfaction with both West Ham and Tottenham's bids.

'All the press coverage has centred on West Ham moaning at Spurs for trying to muscle in on their territory,' Murph said angrily as he signed his name, 'and not once has it mentioned anything about West Ham doing the same to Orient.'

'I can't honestly see why Spurs want to move over here,' I said. 'For a start the fans won't have it. It must be something to do with the new stadium development up in Tottenham. Maybe they're looking for leverage?'

'It's always been West Ham's bid that they want because they promised to keep the track,' Murph said.

'Tracks in football stadia are shit,' Chas scoffed. 'Look at the Stadio delle Alpi in Turin. The atmosphere was like a ghost town and Juventus have moved out.'

We continued discussing the implications of the Olympic Stadium while supping pints in the sanctity of the Supporters Club. Outside, there was a heavy police presence. Sheffield Wednesday had brought a large following, unsurprising given the size of the club. Among their support was our mate Neil. He was a perfect example of a long-suffering football fan who, in almost three decades, has seen his club go through it all. Wednesday had been ever-present in the early years of the Premier League and graced a FA Cup final until the turn of the century when, as is typical in modern football, debts mounted. Like their Yorkshire counterparts Leeds United, their financial instability eventually dragged them down the leagues. The lower divisions are a graveyard littered with teams that have lived the Premier League dream but either failed to capitalise or pushed too far too quickly and imploded.

Neil joined us for the pre-match pints but scuttled off to the away end once the match kicked off. Jamie was running as late as ever, although this time it was for less nefarious reasons. He had decided to run the Paris marathon and had gone on a seven-mile run that morning.

The ground was as packed as I'd ever seen it. The Wednesday fans filled the entire East Stand, much the same as Leeds United's fans had done the year before. A fat shirtless bloke, who I later found out from Neil was called Tango, was orchestrating the chanting and holding his hands high above his bald head.

Wednesday were underachieving in the division for a club of their size and were floating around mid-table, so we expected the match to be a close one. They had the better of the opening exchanges and Orient only went in at half-time with a clean sheet because of a spectacular goal line clearance from Charlie Daniels. 'Ooh Charlie Daniels, ooh Charlie Daniels, ooh Charlie Daniels!' the crowd sang appreciatively as the left-back picked himself up off the floor.

The match burst to life minutes into the second half when Owls' midfielder Gary Teale clearly handled in the area. The Tommy Johnston Stand rose to its feet in outrage, followed quickly by joy as the ref pointed to the spot. Ben Chorley stepped up and confidently tucked the penalty past Nicky Weaver. Minutes later we were on our feet again as Harry Kane, another loanee from Spurs, finished neatly from inside the box to make it 2-0.

The away side was visibly shocked and Orient, sensing blood, pressed home their advantage. Alex Revell leapt high to beat Weaver with a header from a Daniels cross and M'Poku rounded off the rout with a well struck free kick that beat the wall low across the ground and skidded into the net. 4-0.

We couldn't quite believe what we were witnessing. This was how Orient could play. We had seen it in glimpses during the season, but when they really hit their groove, they proved an irresistible force.

'Fat bloke what's the score, fat bloke fat bloke what's the score?' we sang at Tango, who to his credit, took it all in good spirit and rubbed his rotund belly in reply. The Wednesday fans filed out well before the final whistle, which eventually arrived to great cheers of delight from the home crowd.

I called Neil as we left the ground to go back to the Supporters Club. 'Alright mate!' I said down the phone. 'Are you coming for a pint with the victorious Orient boys?'

'I was considering sneaking back 'ome,' he said deject-edly, 'but I suppose I'll come and face the caning from you boys.'

<u>Tuesday 25th January 2011</u>
<u>Orient v MK Dons</u>

It turned out to be a not-so-happy Burn's Night for Scottish pundit Andy Gray. He and his Sky colleague Richard Keys had been caught making off-camera sexist remarks about assistant referee Sian Massey.

'Somebody better get down there and explain offside to her,' Keys was recorded saying during a game between Wolverhampton Wanderers and Liverpool.

'Yeah, I know,' Gray agreed. 'Can you believe that? A female linesman! Women don't know the offside rule.'

'The game's gone mad,' Keys finished.

Gray and Keys had been an integral part of Sky Sports since its football coverage began in the early nineties. They were ever-present on Sunday and Monday night coverage, and many considered them to be sacred cows at the Sky studios. As the days went by, more footage of their misogyny hit the airwaves, including footage of Richard Keys asking an embarrassed Jamie Redknapp if he'd 'smashed' a particular female they were discussing. By Tuesday, the pressure from the press and public to dispense with the two dinosaurs hit a tipping point. Gray was fired.

We were in the Supporters Club ahead of a match with MK Dons, a fixture that was originally frozen out on Boxing Day. Some Sky reporters had been allowed in and were going around the room interviewing supporters about the Olympic Stadium issue. Murph didn't waste the chance for a bit of well-timed satire, asking the female presenter if she understood the offside rule.

As we laughed, Chas stopped and peered through a crowd of people. 'Is that Ray Houghton?' he asked.

Sure enough, the former Liverpool, Aston Villa and Republic of Ireland ace was stood with a couple of Orient fans enjoying a quiet drink. Not wanting to miss the opportunity to speak to a legend of the game, we asked for a quick photo. He kindly obliged and answered our questions. It turned out a good friend of his was an Orient fan and he came along on the odd occasion to enjoy a bit of football.

'If Orient win tonight,' Murph asked with a cheeky grin, 'are you going to celebrate with a roly-poly?'

Murph was referring to Houghton's reaction to a spectacular match-winning strike against Italy in the

1994 World Cup. After smashing a 20-yard effort over the head of Italian keeper Gianluca Pagliuca, Houghton peeled away with arms raised and performed a forward roll before being mobbed by his team mates.

The Dons set off at a furious pace and took an early lead with a strike Ray Houghton would have been proud of. Scott McGleish pulled Orient level moments later following a defensive slip, and Orient completed a quick turnaround when Terrell Forbes out-jumped his marker from a corner and buried a header past the Dons keeper. Fifteen minutes gone, three goals scored.

Orient continued to pile on the pressure and should have grabbed a third when Dean Cox's superb effort crashed against the upright. Charlie Daniels followed up with a surging run and a shot that was well saved. Orient were rampant and looked in imperious form, playing some exciting football. After the thrashing we'd dished out against Wednesday, we hoped for more goals after half-time.

It was like a different team emerged from the tunnel after the break. Stephen Dawson limped off with a dead leg and his replacement, young Harry Kane, a forward rather than a midfielder, failed to add the bite that our departed skipper usually gave us. The passing became sloppy and the pressure our midfield had been exerting throughout the first half all but disappeared.

I glanced at the bench and saw that the usually imposing figure of Russell Slade was absent. 'Where's Slade?' I asked. No-one knew. With Slade missing and Dawson off the field, Orient were missing their heart and soul, and it showed.

The Dons equalised from a corner and it took a sterling effort from the defence for the remainder of the game to keep the score as it was. We trudged off at full-time totally deflated by the result. The first-half dominance should have seen us well ahead, but we returned to the bad old days of earlier in the season. Two points dropped. How crucial would they be at the end of the season?

Two days later, I was back on the Central Line to Newbury Park for another Orient trip. This time, I was meeting Chas at 11:30 for our visit to the training ground. To record the occasion, Chas had his sister's camcorder and I had Stace's new Nikon camera, covered in buttons and gizmos which I had no idea how to use properly.

Orient train at the Ford Sport and Social Club within Seven Kings Park. It was a freezing cold day, and as we turned the corner and began to follow the long driveway to the clubhouse, a bitter wind swept across the field and into our faces. Small groups of players were passing a ball back and forth over to our right, a larger group was practising corner routines in a set of goals further across the field.

We were met by Howard Gould, the club's community liaison officer, who welcomed us at the gates and talked us through what was going on. He told us the first team players were happy to help out and were just in the process of showering and changing after a training session.

He led us down a long dark-grey corridor. It smelled of wet grass and deep-heat spray and was filled with steam from the showers that hissed loudly from rooms to our left and right. The voices of players could be heard joking and laughing above the noise of the gushing water behind half-open doors of changing rooms. It was a vivid reminder of my time as a junior club player.

We entered a large room with a wooden dance floor beneath a high, flat roof. The players were gathered around small tables on a carpeted area at the far end. Through patio doors beyond them were pitches dotted in cones.

Dean Cox, Alex Revell and Jimmy Smith were sat at one table, next to them were Stephen Dawson, Matt Spring, Charlie Daniels and newly-signed right-back Andrew Whing. Scott McGleish stood over them cracking jokes. Alone in the far corner, quietly eating his lunch, was Russell Slade.

'This is proper random,' I whispered to Chas as we crossed the dance floor to a table and chairs. Howard suggested we set up our equipment there.

'I know mate,' he whispered back. 'Murph is going to be gutted he missed this!'

Chas inserted a fresh disc into the camera and I fiddled with Stace's Nikon, pretending I knew what I was doing. I was trying to pluck up the courage to approach the players. Thankfully, Howard broke the ice for us.

'OK lads, this is Charles and Adam, a couple of O's fans, and they'd like you to give a little message for their mate who's getting married.'

'When's da wedd'n?' Dawson asked us in his broad Irish accent.

'Err, not 'til the end of July,' I replied.

'So what kind of thing are you after?' said the gravelly voice of McGleish.

'Maybe,' Revell cut in, 'we could all say how well we all knew... what's the bride's name?'

'Danielle,' Chas said.

'OK,' Revell continued mischievously, 'we could all say how well we knew Danielle and what a lovely girl she is. Know what I mean?'

'I'm not sure showing a video that implies half the Orient team has shagged the bride is quite the angle we were going for,' I said, laughing.

We established a quick script and lined the players up against the back wall of the hall. I gave them a quick introduction and then handed over to the players.

It was Scott McGleish that did the honours. 'Anthony and Danielle, congratulations on your wedding day from all of us here, we hope you have a good day... and Anthony, have you smashed it yet?'

The players cheered at the last line, which that morning had been responsible for removing Richard Keys from his job at Sky. Chas and I were left in fits of laughter and wondering how well that would go down at the wedding in the summer.

We hung around for a while chatting with the players. They had a team meeting once lunch was over, prior to their trip to Swansea the following day for the FA Cup tie on Saturday. McGleish and I had a long conversation about the coming fixture in Wales. He told me how funny he finds it when he takes his wife and young son to games and we sing the 'he's here, he's there, he's every-fucking-where' song after he scores. His son excitedly sings it back to him after matches, innocently leaving out the swear words.

Russell Slade came over and gave a short wedding message for us, doffing his cap in trademark fashion. He was the embodiment of patience as we messed around with the camera trying to set it up. Bidding the players goodbye and good luck for the weekend, we headed outside to do some introductory shots so we could edit it together at a later date.

It began snowing as we walked back towards the station. With the fun out of the way, I had no distraction from Nanna's funeral the following day. My mum asked me if I would do the eulogy. I didn't know what to write and whether or not I'd make it through the reading without breaking down. It took a lot of reassurance from Stace to get me through it.

Once it was written, I read it through a hundred times. Now I just wanted to deliver it and for the day to be over. It passed quickly. I spent much of the ceremony preceding my eulogy comforting my cousin and Stacey, who both got very teary as we followed Nanna's coffin, festooned in West Ham colours, down towards the altar.

It wasn't until after I delivered my address and Nanna's coffin had been taken slowly back out of the church to the first few bars of the final hymn that I broke down. I walked out behind my family trying to cover my tears with my hands, ashamed that my emotions had got the better of me.

At the burial site I broke down again as my grandad knelt down at the grave to give his final goodbye to the woman who had been his wife for 63 years. Watching a usually-stoic old man mourning the loss of his soulmate was a heartbreaking moment.

We had a cheery wake back at my grandparents' house where everyone sat around talking and laughing normally. It was a fitting celebration of my nan's life that the family she treasured beyond anything else was relaxing, side-by-side, enjoying each other's company.

My dad drove Stacey and I from Hutton afterwards, but we didn't go straight home. Stace and I had been discussing buying a property for some time but lacked the money required for a deposit. My dad, ever the frugal Scotsman, hated seeing us throw good money away on rent. He suggested we go and visit some estate agents in Wanstead, an area we were keen on moving to, to see what properties were on offer. It was a strange turn of events after such an emotional day, but a sign that families must move on.

I felt exhausted by emotion and I was ready to have a bit of a blow out with the lads to shake off some of the blues. We had decided not to bother making the trek to Swansea for the FA Cup tie because the Welsh-language channel S4C was televising the game.

Instead, I spent a couple of the hours it would have taken to travel to Wales writing an email about the Olympic Stadium bid and how it affected Orient, and sent it to London Mayor Boris Johnson, former Mayor Ken Livingstone and football writer and West Ham fan Martin Samuel. I felt I needed to air my views to the right people. Whether I would get a response was another matter.

We met at Murph's house in South Woodford at midday for the 12:50 kick-off. Chas and Joss were already there, along with Finch, who was back from China where he had been teaching for the past six months. Finch was a Spurs fan and had been a pretty regular companion of mine at White Hart Lane for a while.

Jamie arrived just after kick-off, just in time to join us in cracking open the first cans of the afternoon. The insights Scott McGleish had offered on Thursday proved true. As he predicted, Stephen Dawson started the game after his dead leg against MK Dons, but he was heavily strapped.

The Liberty Stadium looked empty. Aside from the familiar chants of the Orient fans tucked away out of shot, there was very little noise at all. Orient were doing well to hang on as the Swans, flying high in the Championship, dominated the game.

With 35 minutes gone, however, Charlie Daniels swung in a free kick from the right. The keeper rushed to punch clear but Jimmy Smith got there first and glanced a header into the back of the net. We all went mad, jumping from our seats and leaping around Murph's front room, while Danielle looked on, horrified we might break something.

The hosts drew level just before half-time after Orient failed to clear their lines. A ball knocked deep into the box was met by a Swansea head and guided into the top corner.

The second half was much the same as the first. Like the Norwich match at the start of the month, Orient were defending for their lives and hoping for a lucky break that might snatch an unlikely win. Lucky is what we got. With just a couple of minutes remaining, M'Poku shimmied back and forth at the edge of the box and passed a hopeful ball towards the front post. A Swansea defender running across to cover it swung his boot to clear the danger but only succeeded in slicing it past his flummoxed goalkeeper.

For a second, no-one realised what happened. As soon as we spotted red shirts running towards M'Poku in celebration and heard the faint roar of the Orient support, we erupted in cheers. The final few minutes ticked away and we endured another anxious wait until at last the final whistle blew and we exploded into wild celebrations once more. Orient had reached the FA Cup fifth round for the first time since 1982, before I was even born!

We hit Wanstead to celebrate, anticipating the possibility of a home tie against one of the big guns in the draw the following day. Arsenal and Man United were still in the draw, although Spurs would bow out the next day at the hands of Fulham.

Feeling slightly the worse for wear after waking up fully-clothed on the sofa at 5am, Stace dragged me shopping on Sunday. My phone bleeped in my pocket. I whooped in delight when I read Chas' message, causing some strange looks from my fellow patrons in Sainsbury's on Whitechapel Road. 'Unbelievable! We drew Arsenal at home!!! Don't know what I'm gonna do!'

Arsenal at Brisbane Road. What a quirk of fate. Murph and Chas would have their allegiances tested to the full, but I could relish a fairytale FA Cup draw, an incredible reward for battling displays against Norwich and Swansea. To think Orient were just two minutes from going out against Droylsden. Now I had two reasons to hate Arsenal.

```
13.Exeter City.........P26|W9 |D8 |L9 |F37|A43|35pts
14.Hartlepool United...P25|W9 |D7 |L9 |F27|A35|34pts
15.Plymouth Argyle.....P28|W9 |D6 |L13|F35|A46|33pts
16.Leyton Orient.......P24|W8 |D8 |L8 |F38|A36|32pts
17.Brentford...........P26|W6 |D5 |L12|F30|A34|32pts
18.Notts County........P24|W9 |D4 |L11|F31|A31|31pts
19.Swindon Town........P27|W7 |D9 |L11|F37|A44|30pts
```

February 2011

The mid-season transfer deadline passed in a flurry of activity. January's transfer window is often used in a make-or-break attempt to strengthen squads for a final push for glory or for a relegation scrap. The desperation in certain deals is reflected in the fees that are paid, and this year was no different. Liverpool, who were striving to get back into the Champions League qualifying spots, purchased Newcastle United's giant forward Andy Carroll for £35 million and Ajax's Uruguayan striker Luis Suarez for £22 million. Suarez, prolific for his club, had been a revelation at the World Cup and his fee was probably a fair reflection of his growing status. Carroll's fee, on the other hand, was an incredible sum for a young player, very much a target man rather than goal scorer, who had only played once for his country at senior level and who was carrying an injury. Overnight he became the most expensive British footballer of all time and the eighth most expensive in the history of football.

He replaced Fernando Torres on Merseyside. After a mediocre season and with speculation surrounding his future, the Spaniard moved to Chelsea for £50 million, much to the chagrin of the Reds' supporters. To pay such an exorbitant amount of money for a player who was out of sorts for a year, plagued by injuries and who had netted just half a dozen times in the league was a huge gamble for the Blues. With Russian billionaire Roman Abramovich bankrolling the club they could comfortably afford it, but the expense and extravagance of spending £50 million on one player was symbolic of what the Premier League had become.

Spurs were surprisingly inactive in the final hours despite their glaringly obvious need for a striker. Midnight passed and White Hart Lane remained silent, despite their attempts throughout the month to splash ridiculous amounts of cash on players like Sergio Aguero, Diego Forlan and Giuseppe Rossi.

Avoiding the relapse that overcame me in August's final transfer flurry, I was apathetic to the supposed drama unfolding throughout the day. I abandoned the running live feeds on the Sky and the BBC websites, ignored Twitter and paid no attention to Jim White on Sky Sports News.

The only update I was interested in came via email from Chas and Murph. They passed on the news that

Jason Crowe, a utility defender, had signed for Orient from Leeds. I was excited by the news, recalling his outstanding performance against Manchester United in the FA Cup a season ago. He was exactly the type of player we needed if we were to shore up the defence and continue to march up the league.

<u>Tuesday 1st February 2011</u>
<u>Orient v Brighton & Hove Albion</u>

Just a month after our drubbing at the hands of league leaders Brighton, the clubs met again. I whiled away the tedious hours at work before the match reading irate rants from unhappy Spurs fans on blogs across the internet. Most said the same thing: 'where's the striker we need 'Arry?' I agreed with them, but I refused to let it bother me. Spurs were set for the rest of the season, so no use moaning.

Orient's upcoming cup tie with Arsenal had the media buzzing around the club. Articles appeared online and in the press about the club. Barry Hearn called in to Mark Chapman's *Premier League Podcast* and spoke at length about the club's achievement in the cup, the excitement ahead of the Arsenal game and the fears he held for the future of the club with the Olympic Stadium decision looming.

I couldn't help but think it a strange coincidence that in the one season I picked to start following the O's they were splashed all over the news for all sorts of reasons. The players had even done an advert for the Nintendo DS. From obscurity they were becoming ubiquitous. Maybe they had always been there in some way or another and it was only when I started looking that I noticed them. It was great to see the club getting the exposure, but was it the beginning of the slippery slope to the hype and over-financing that had crippled the Premier League?

I met the others at Leyton station at 6pm and was amazed at the numbers of people making their way to the ground so early.

'Where have all these people come from?' I asked as we made our way down the High Road to the ground.

'Did you not read the club website?' Murph replied. 'Supporters who have ticket stubs from tonight and the Swindon game next Tuesday will get priority on Arsenal cup tickets.'

'Genius!' I said with a laugh. 'You can say what you like about Barry Hearn, but he's as shrewd as they come!'

Sure enough, the roads around the stadium were packed and the queues at the ticket office stretched down the road. The Supporters Club was full. The FA Cup was already having a positive impact on the club's coffers and the big game itself was still a couple of weeks away.

Fighting to get to the bar, we squeezed ourselves into a corner. At the front doors, Scott McGleish was being presented with a bottle of bubbly for a man of the match performance in a previous game. We all cheered and started singing his song.

163

'What's going on?' a bloke asked me, craning his neck to peer across the crowded room at what was happening.

'Scotty's getting his man of the match award,' I said, clapping my hands as McGleish took a humble bow of appreciation and left for the changing rooms.

'Who's that then?' he said, looking puzzled.

'Scott McGleish,' I said, pausing for some reaction before adding, 'our striker?'

'Oh,' he said nodding, 'the Scottish guy.'

'Err, no.'

'How long has he been here then?'

'McGleish? Years!' I said incredulously.

'Oh, right,' he said looking sheepish. 'I've got no idea to be honest, I'm just here with a mate.' With that he turned and headed towards the bar.

Clearly he was one of the many 'supporters' here for the ticket stub rather than the match. Probably an Arsenal fan too. It was typical of the evening. Unfamiliar faces and an overcrowded bar suggested that many of those present weren't interested in tonight's game. It made me wonder why, if they were willing to spend £40 on two Tuesday night fixtures just to obtain the right to spend another £20 on a one-off game against Arsenal, they couldn't come down and support the club more often?

Extricating ourselves from the busy bar, we made our way to the seats. Paul and his mates who sit behind us were struggling to hang a huge banner from the back of the corrugated stand with a roll of duct tape. Once unfurled and suspended fully, the banner read: 'NO FOOTBALL WITHOUT THE O's!'

It was a clear message about the Olympic Stadium. This was our club and killing it would be a strike at the heart of football itself.

The first half passed with few chances. Brighton looked pretty ordinary despite their lofty position in the league. The crowd, topped up with day-tripping Arsenal fans and a healthy travelling support from the south coast, looked to top 6,000. It was all money in the club's coffers.

The second half was little better, although Orient were definitely the ones on top and perhaps could have nicked the win. The passion of the team was evident and almost came to boiling point when Cox and M'Poku had some crossed words and a bit of a tangle over who was going to take a free kick. Compared to the limp performances earlier in the season it was good to see the players had some fire in their belly, even over something as trivial as a set piece.

The game ended 0-0. Considering the scoreline at the Withdean a month before, it was a decent result and kept our run of unbeaten home games going. One thing that did stand out was the standard of officiating. The referee and both of his assistants had a night to forget, and both sides were left aggrieved by some quite ludicrous decisions. I was getting quite used to the poor standards of the officials, having suffered at their hands all season.

The next few days were taken up by house-hunting. I had persuaded Stace that the best place for us to buy was in Leyton or Leytonstone. We would still be on the Central Line, just like our original favoured destination in Wanstead. Anywhere closer to the city was way out of our price range. With Stratford already the focus of regeneration because of the Olympics, Leyton and Leytonstone would be a wise investment for future resale. The close proximity to Orient was a happy bonus that Stace didn't immediately pick up on.

We had already gone through the oddly grown-up experience of discussing a mortgage with an advisor in Wanstead and viewing a couple of properties, neither of which sparked any enthusiasm. The advice we were given was to not rush and go for the first one you see.

As it was, it was the third property, situated in Whipps Cross near Leytonstone, which struck a chord. After discussing it for all of thirty seconds, moments after saying goodbye to the current owners who had just showed us around, we called the agents and made a bid.

'Adam,' Stace said after she had finished the call, 'we just made an offer for a house!' I smiled and flung an arm over her shoulders.

'Yep, looks like you're going to be stuck with me, doesn't it?'

<u>Tuesday 8th February 2011</u>
<u>Orient v Swindon Town</u>

The excitement didn't last. The ups and downs (and there are more downs than ups) of buying a property were hammered home when I received a teary phone call from Stace one afternoon, informing me our bid had been rejected and someone else's offer accepted.

'That's the way it goes,' I said philosophically, disguising my own disappointment. 'Something better will come along. Don't worry about it.'

After reflecting on the situation and trawling through various property websites, I set off for Orient's game against Swindon in defiant mood. Something better would come along. As a football supporter I'm used to facing disappointment but know full well there's often something positive waiting just around the corner.

The Supporters Club was packed again and the queues at the ticket office were once more snaking down the road. Unlike the bloke's attempt to bluff his way in the Supporters Club the week before, this time Arsenal fans seemed to be far more open in their motives. Two were even discussing where they sat at the Emirates Stadium while they stood at the bar waiting to be served.

Although I was far from a seasoned Orient fan and made no secret of my true allegiance to Spurs, I couldn't help but feel cynical about these fans. It was a brief flirtation that would be done away with once the Arsenal game was over. I was here for the long haul.

In reality, most were probably genuinely passionate Arsenal fans, like so many others, who had been priced out of their club and this was the one rare opportunity they had to see the Gunners in action. Perhaps it may even lead to them giving the O's a go on a more permanent basis, spawning a whole new interest in a different club. With the possibility of gaining new fans and Orient receiving a much-needed financial boost from increased ticket sales, it was a win-win for all concerned and a shining example of why the FA Cup is still such an important and cherished competition.

The atmosphere inside the ground was excellent, just as it had been the week before. Although Orient were on a great run of form and rescued a point away at Bournemouth with a last-minute equaliser at the weekend, they started this match dreadfully. Swindon knocked the ball around nicely and looked far more composed. Nothing was clicking for the O's and the regulars amongst us started to become a little impatient. Then – bang, bang, bang – Orient were 3-0 up. Cox drove a free kick beneath a jumping wall to open the scoring, leaving the Swindon goalkeeper apoplectic with rage at his defenders. Revell followed up on a parried close-range header to make it two, and then Orient, who had been struggling all night to string passes together, cut majestically through a shell-shocked Robin's defence. The ball was back-heeled to Dawson who glided past one man, darted along the edge of the box and fired back across the keeper from eighteen yards and into the net. It was wonderful stuff. The crowd were up and applauding and singing the captain's name. If this didn't make those casual fans want to come back for more then nothing would.

The second half saw a succession of half-chances at both ends. Apart from Jamie Jones making a terrific save from a Swindon free kick, the keepers remained untroubled. With fifteen minutes of the game remaining, hundreds of satisfied Arsenal fans streamed out of the ground clutching their valuable ticket stubs.

'You're only here for the Arsenal, here for the Arrrrsenal!' we sang with derision at the departing crowds, with the Swindon fans joining the chorus. A few acknowledged this with a wave and a thumbs up which added some amusement to the farcical scenes before a new chant of 'stand up for the Orient' began to echo around the stands and we rose to our feet in response.

On leaving the ground at the final whistle, it was clear to see why so many had left early. The cup tickets had gone on sale the moment the referee had blown for full-time and a long queue had formed from the Oliver Road ticket office, around the corner onto Buckingham Road and tailed off into the distance towards High Road. With our tickets already safely purchased the week before, season tickets giving us priority, we followed the line down to the main road and headed back up to the station. The cup game should be one to remember.

My birthday on Thursday was greeted by pouring rain. I took the day off so Stace and I could spend my first afternoon as a 28-year-old slipping around the wet streets of Leytonstone looking at houses.

From the tube station we trudged off through the downpour to meet an agent at the first of three properties we were seeing that day, all less than a fifteen-minute walk from Brisbane Road. We fell in love with the first place almost immediately, casting knowing smiles and glances at each other as the agent showed us each room. After seeing the other two properties, we retired to a restaurant opposite the station to dry off and discuss what we had seen.

It was settled in an instant, we wanted the first and we would stop at nothing to get it. Something better had indeed come along, and it seemed fitting that we found it on my birthday. We made an offer the second we left the restaurant, going in at under the asking price but not so much as to be dismissed out of hands. Now all we could do was wait.

The next day was D-Day for the Olympic Stadium decision. Not good news for Orient. West Ham were chosen as the successful bidders, and now all that was needed was for the government and the Mayor of London to rubber stamp the proposal. Barry Hearn and Spurs chairman Daniel Levy immediately went on the offensive and vowed to challenge the decision that, according to the Olympic Park Legacy Committee, 'Londoners wanted'. It was a statement that could not have been further from the truth.

It was a funny state of affairs to have the two clubs I supported arm-in-arm, although for entirely different motives, fighting the club that had provided me with my first experience of football. The whole situation was a tangled mess and one that the 2012 Olympic Committee had to shoulder the blame for. Despite West Ham's delight, with pressure from the press and suggestions that it would go to court, the decision was already looking shaky.

<u>Saturday 12th February 2011</u>
<u>Orient v Bristol Rovers</u>

There were only two topics of conversation in the Supporters Club at the weekend: Arsenal and the Olympic Stadium. We arrived early to cover both while watching the Manchester derby which was lit up by a wonder goal from Rooney, acrobatically volleying a bicycle kick past Joe Hart from a deep cross to win the match 2-1.

On the way to our seats, Stace phoned to ask if I'd heard anything about the house. We chatted briefly and then I let her know I would be staying around after the game to watch the Spurs game on the TV.

'Love you!' I said, finishing the call.

'Yeah, bye,' she replied and hung up the phone.

I stared at my silent phone for a couple of seconds, confused by the abrupt manner in which Stace ended the conversation, but with a shrug of the shoulders I pocketed my phone and settled into my seat. Perhaps I had been neglecting her a bit recently. I had been to a lot of games in a short space of time. I was stewing on this as Orient opened the scoring through Jimmy Smith with virtually the first attack of the game.

Sitting back in my seat I fired off a message to Stace. 'I say I love you and you say yeah bye. Not a very nice way to sign off. Love you and I'm sorry that recently it's been like this but it's just the way it is xxx.'

Stuffing my phone back into my pocket, thinking that should do the trick and Stacey would realise why I'd been away so much, I turned my attention back to the game. Orient were 1-0 up and cruising. Their dominance was rewarded from an unlikely source as right-back Andrew Whing crashed in a thunderous shot from 25 yards out into the top corner.

Bouncing around with delight, I felt my phone buzz in my pocket. Stace had sent me an essay length riposte to what I now realised was a lame effort in placating her.

'Sorry. It's just upsetting that I have to sit at home every weekend as I have no money while you're out every weekend drinking with your mates. If it was the other way around I'd sacrifice a weekend and take you out instead. It would be nice if you thought, Stacey must be a bit fed up, I'll take her to the cinema. It's also upsetting that you want to spend your birthday weekend doing something you do every weekend instead of doing something with me. Makes me feel so shit. Especially as I'm so upset and stressed about the house.'

I started to feel bad now, but the dates of football fixtures were not my fault. I fired off another text saying as much and put my phone away until half-time. On checking it again at the interval, I realised the row had escalated.

'You don't seem to understand why I'm so upset. The issue is that you are out every Saturday night.'

The text fight continued back and forth, with me accusing her of demanding I come home right away, and her saying I should *want* to come home. I was annoyed and totally distracted from the game. Was this my fault? Was I being selfish and neglecting my girlfriend for football and pints with the lads? Perhaps it was just the nerves of waiting on the house that was causing this little outburst.

I decided to ignore my phone for the rest of the game. I was in a bad mood, distracted from the match, and Orient seemed to mirror me. With a lapse in concentration, they gifted Bristol Rovers a lifeline as Ben Chorley put through his own goal.

Thankfully, it was jut a minor wobble as second-half substitute Harry Kane netted twice to round off what was a very comfortable win. Having almost entirely forgotten about the disagreement with Stace, we relocated to the King Harold on the High Road to watch Spurs take on Sunderland and play a bit of darts.

Sunderland opened the scoring, much to Joss's delight, but just before half-time Spurs grabbed an equaliser. 'Youse'll probably go on an win it now,' Joss said with a grimace, 'we've bin playin' shite at home recently. Typical Sunderland. Always play shite after Christmas.'

Spurs did indeed find the net a second time, but I didn't see it. I realised far too late that I was well and truly in the wrong with Stacey. She was upset, stressed and alone and I was out having a good time. What leg did I have to stand on? I would need to address the problem sooner rather than later or I wouldn't so much be looking for a new house as I would a new girlfriend.

I knew it would be tough balancing what are essentially two relationships. Like two opposing tectonic plates, your partner and your football team rub along fine most of the time but occasionally they hit a snag that sends tremors through you. Arguments and disagreements like this must erupt all over the country every week. Supporting a football club requires commitment in the same way a loving relationship does, although Orient wouldn't make me sleep on the couch if I failed to turn up to a game. It takes a lot of understanding on both sides to make it work. I hoped these were just teething problems while we both adjusted to things in my first season as a season ticket holder.

I made my excuses and left, walking as fast as I could back to the station. I arrived at home drenched to the bone, looking apologetic and clutching a bunch of flowers from Tesco. I had seen the error of my ways and had redeemed myself, for the time being at least.

Along with the stresses of following two football teams and buying a house, I had the added pressure of my employment status to consider. The interview I had attended after Christmas must have gone well because I was put forward for the next round of the process. I had to give a presentation about a fictional new product that the company was considering adding to its portfolio. Having little experience giving presentations since my schooldays and no idea what product I could invent, I turned to my dad for some guidance. After much work and preparation I felt ready. I set off dressed in a suit that had inexplicably shrunk around the middle since the last time I had worn it.

Fighting off the nerves, I entered the boardroom. Six faces smiled at me in welcome. After a brief explanation of the session's format, I was off and away. Once I got into my stride, things flowed very naturally. Either I impressed the panel or they were very good actors. Whether I had done enough would remain to be seen. I left the interview buzzing and didn't come down from the adrenaline rush until later on that evening. Now I was waiting on two sets of news: a job and a house.

I tried to forget about both as Spurs played in the Champions League last sixteen against AC Milan. As usual I had no Sky Sports, but disastrously the internet connection failed. I resorted to sitting watching the score on my phone for the entire match, refreshing the page every couple of minutes.

Orient were playing too, away at MK Dons. The Dons went a goal up, only to be pegged back by another Jimmy Smith goal. MK then took a 2-1 lead but Smith, on fire in front of goal in recent games, popped up for a second time to level the scores.

Spurs were enjoying some good spells of possession, at least according to the text updates. With ten minutes gone it was still 0-0, already surpassing their last outing at the San Siro when Inter bagged three early goals. As the game reached the final ten minutes, it remained scoreless.

My finger nails had been chewed down to a bloody nub. I hit refresh for the thousandth time and whooped in delight. Peter Crouch had scored.

Five minutes before Crouch struck, Jonathan Téhoué had put Orient into the lead. A win away at MK Dons would be a great result, and for Spurs, a win in the San Siro against the giants of AC Milan would be incredible.

I sat nervously awaiting the full-time whistles in Milton Keynes and Milan. Finally they came. I flicked on Sky Sports News to see Spurs celebrating and Milan's feisty midfielder Gennaro Gatusso going nose-to-nose with Spurs' first-team coach Joe Jordan on the touchline. The little Italian and the big Scot were fiercely conversing in pidgin Glaswegian and Milanese, before Gattuso's temper cracked and he butted Jordan across the nose. A melee of bodies piled in to break up the warring parties and the players were lead from the field.

Buoyed by the interview and the fantastic results both teams had achieved on the same night, the run of good fortune continued. The following day, sat staring at a computer screen at work, my phone rang. It was Stace.

'Adam,' she said, failing to hide the glee in her voice, 'we've just bought a house!'

'What?' I said in amazement. 'The offer was accepted?'

'The vendor said yes to ours despite there being a bigger offer from someone else. They didn't have their finances sorted and she felt we were better prepared to do the deal!'

All we had to do was go through the process of organising the mortgage properly, exchanging contracts and picking a date. We would then own our own little piece of planet earth, a stone's throw from Orient!

I kept in mind that a lot of things could go wrong between acceptance and completion. I wouldn't be counting any chickens yet. If life as a football supporter has taught me anything over the years, it's that what can look nice and rosy one minute can turn into disaster and despair the next.

<u>Sunday 20th February 2011</u>
<u>Orient v Arsenal</u>

The big day arrived: FA Cup fifth round. The Orient-Arsenal match had been chosen for TV broadcast and kicked off late in the afternoon, but we planned to make a day of it.

I met Jamie on Brick Lane at 12:15 and we headed over to Liverpool Street. Transport for London had picked the biggest day Orient had seen for the past thirty years to undertake engineering works on the Central Line, meaning we and everyone else coming from central London would need to go overground to Stratford and then take a bus or walk one mile to the stadium.

We chose to walk it, passing the Olympic Park on our journey on the left hand side. It was a grey, cold day, and in those bleak conditions we found it hard to see how the Olympics would do much to improve what was a very deprived and run down area of London.

We arrived to a surprisingly busy Supporters Club given that it was still a few hours from kick-off. Other fans had chosen to make a day of it as we had. Chas was wearing a commemorative scarf with both Orient and Arsenal badges woven into it.

'Perfect scarf for you, Chas,' I said turning it over to see both sides.

'So who are you supporting today then?' Jamie enquired.

'Well, it's hard to choose. It'd be great if Orient won, amazing really, but who's more likely to go on and actually win the cup?' Chas answered.

'So there's no competition for you today then is there?' Jamie said flipping Chas's scarf around to display the Arsenal side.

'Shut up,' Chas said, rearranging the scarf. 'I know you lot are just on the wind up.'

'So why aren't you wearing your Orient shirt today then Chas?' Murph said, looking up at the big man enquiringly.

Chas shot him a knowing and withering glare. 'Don't you bloody start, you're in the same situation that I am.'

As we continued baiting Chas over his allegiances, Joss arrived to complete our quintet and joined a rapidly-filling bar. We watched Manchester City take on Notts County in a one-sided fourth round game that had originally been postponed because of the weather, and then with last orders called ahead of the game we headed into the ground.

We dived into the Tommy Johnston Stand bar for a final quick pint to guarantee our vocal chords were nicely lubricated and were confronted by a sea of people packed in wall-to-wall. As we drank, the sixth round draw took place on the screens dotted around the bar. Everyone was shouting for Manchester United away, as though Orient had already disposed of the first Premier League giant to cross our paths.

The balls were pulled one by one from the pot with no sign of either Orient or Man United emerging. When the third from last ball was drawn and still neither side had emerged, a huge roar went up. The roar turned into bedlam as United's ball was drawn first. The air was filled with whoops and cheers and beer showered down over us. Old Trafford here we come!

The match was a sell-out, which meant 9,300 people were packed into Brisbane Road. We climbed the steps to the stand, emerging in a cacophony of noise, and immediately joined in the songs. With the television cameras in attendance and the world watching from their sofas, the supporters had chosen this as their stage to mount their vocal protest over the Olympic Stadium decision.

'Chim-chimeny, chim-chimeny, chim-chim-cheroo, we hate those bastards in claret and blue!'

All kinds of new songs emerged, off the cuff it seemed, some of which were pretty unkind to West Ham vice-chairwoman Karren Brady. We even started a few of our own and were delighted to hear then sung back with deafening gusto.

Arsenal fielded a pretty decent eleven considering Arsene Wenger's usual team selections against weaker opposition. The visitors predictably dominated possession, knocking it around in neat triangles as Orient players scampered after them. The Orient crowd was in full voice and barely a soul was left seated. A few half-chances went begging, with Danish international Niklas Bendtner and Moroccan Marouane Chamakh guilty of some wasteful finishing. The half-time whistle was greeted with a huge cheer. Orient survived the first 45 minutes with their goal still intact thanks to some dogged defending and poor finishing.

The chanting and singing subsided for the duration of the half-time break. My throat was starting to feel sore and fifteen minutes respite was a welcome relief. The whistle for the start of the second half was the cue to begin singing again. Murph received a text message from Danielle telling him she could see us on the TV and that the camera kept cutting to us in the stands. We would have to do ourselves justice.

Eight minutes into the second half, our bubble burst. Bendtner, who had received plenty of stick from the home fans, crossed the ball to the far post where Tomas Rosicky headed the ball past Jamie Jones and into the net. The Arsenal fans in the East Stand erupted in noise for the first time in the match, only for chants of 'we forgot that you were here' and 'you only sing when you're winning' to start from the rest of the ground. Among the Orient fans hurling abuse at their Arsenal counterparts were Chas and

Murph, barking insults at their Gooner brethren across the ground.

Almost immediately after the restart, Alex Revell had a headed effort saved by Manuel Almunia. Although Arsenal were the more likely to score and were definitely in the driving seat, at 1-0 anything was possible.

The noise continued and I was almost hoarse. Arsenal pressed for the killer goal and Jamie Jones made two inspired saves in quick succession. Russian forward Andrei Arshavin looked to have clinched it when his angled shot beat everyone, only for it to strike the foot of the post and go harmlessly wide.

Darkness fell and I was unaware of the time or how long was left. It was clear from the anxious faces around me that there was not long to go. Just a couple of minutes of normal time.

Orient took a quick free kick just inside Arsenal's half. M'Poku took up the ball and ran at his man, laying it off to fellow Spurs loanee Tom Carroll. He clipped the ball into the Arsenal back four, who easily headed clear. The ball fell kindly back to Carroll who flung a leg at it and found Jonathan Téhoué 25 yards from goal. The Frenchman brought it down, turned, shimmied and ran at two defenders. Bursting between them, he broke clear into the box and surged towards goal.

The crowd in the Tommy Johnston Stand was already on its feet and seemed to take a collective intake of breath. Everything slowed down for an instant, only to pick up speed as the burly striker strode forward and smashed a low drive under Almunia and into the back of the net.

The explosion of joy was incredible. All around Brisbane Road, bodies jumped and writhed in unbridled ecstasy. I leapt with them, grabbing Chas around the shoulders and screaming manically into the night. Murph almost disappeared three rows down as his momentum carried him forward into the tide of fans in front of us. I screamed so loudly in euphoria and with such force it felt as though I would black out. Over to our right, Russell Slade streaked off down the touchline arms aloft. His cap lifted off his head exposing the hairless dome beneath, gleaming in the light of the blazing floodlights.

After what seemed like an eternity, the crowd began to settle back down. The chorus of songs began again, killing the little time that remained before Orient sealed an incredible result.

Finally the whistle blew and the cheers rang out once more. My head felt light on my shoulders from the exertion I'd put my body through for 90 minutes. I was stopped and interviewed by a girl with a small TV camera outside the ground. She asked me about the game, but I could barely get a coherent word out in reply.

We made for the Supporters Club, already alive with noise and laughter. One thing was for certain, we all wanted to be at the Emirates Stadium for the replay. Harry Kane and Stephen Dawson came into the bar to be with their families and we went over to congratulate them on their efforts, along with most of the room. An hour later the chairman Barry Hearn entered the club to a big roar of appreciation. He was handed the microphone. The first of what he said was lost amongst the noise but then he announced, 'we're not giving up either and we're going to the Emirates looking for a bloody result!'

Another huge cheer welcomed this statement. The noise died down and he continued. 'Before I disappear, I just want to say, and I mean this sincerely, this is a big day for all of us, we're gonna be remembering this for the rest of our lives. This is what makes you lot different, and whether I agree or disagree with you most of the time, one thing we are joined in unison on is that we are bloody different, that's for sure. This area survived the Blitz, it survived God knows how much unemployment and recession and we're still in there fighting, and we've got one of our biggest struggles coming up now with West Ham and this stadium...'

A chorus of boos rang out as he mentioned our neighbours across in Newham borough.

'No, no, no,' he contested with a smile, 'we will fight the authorities every inch of the way!'

Another huge cheer, this time accompanied by Chas shouting 'go on Bazza!'

The chairman waited for quiet once more before finishing. 'Now listen, you've heard enough from me, 'ave a knees up, 'ave a party, you all deserve it. Well done!'

With that he turned and headed for the exit to more cheers. Murph and I looked at each other, and without saying a word dashed outside.

'Barry, do you mind if we have a quick photo with you?' Murph asked,

'Of course not lads,' he replied and duly obliged.

'Absolutely champion effort tonight boys,' he said as he shook our hands, as if we'd played the full ninety minutes ourselves.

The bar began to empty, but we remained there until 9:30. Chas somehow found himself stuck in conversation with a chubby girl purporting to be an Arsenal fan. She had him pressed tightly against the bar while we looked over her shoulder making rude gestures and laughing at Chas as he tried to extricate himself from her clutches.

As we made to leave, we were greeted by the sight of Chas and his young lady in the middle of the room in a clinch, snogging furiously. The Supporters Club had probably never seen such a stomach-churning sight before. Looking at each other and cringing, we headed into the night.

The following weekend was quiet. There was no match at Brisbane Road, so I went from the heady delight of seeing Orient hold Arsenal to a draw in the flesh to watching scores slowly update on my laptop. Orient were away at Huddersfield and had fallen two goals behind soon after half-time. The unbeaten run, which stretched back to New Year's Day, was over. Or so I thought. Harry Kane pulled one back before getting himself sent off.

With a few minutes left and the BBC website failing on me, I got a phone call. Murph was screaming down the phone, 'what a goal, what a massive goal!' Orient had equalised with almost the last move of the game. Jimmy Smith had once again risen above all others to nod home, the Tim Cahill of the lower leagues.

Wayne Rooney was back in the news again, once again for all the wrong reasons. After his wonder strike against City earlier in the month, he had let himself down again and would be back in front of the disciplinary committee after elbowing Wigan midfielder James McCarthy. The Man United striker escaped punishment for it on the day but was facing a retrospective suspension. It seemed all Rooney could do was cause controversy. Be it for England or United, his name was never far from the headlines. A lack of goals was plaguing his season and he had been racking up a lengthy charge sheet of offences. For such a talented player and one who young fans and players look to as a role model, his conduct was setting the wrong kind of example.

Arsenal's week didn't improve. Orient's late fightback must have been preying on their minds as they took to the Wembley turf for the League Cup final against Birmingham City. All the build up to the game was typically one-eyed as pundits and fans stepped up to declare that this was the time that Arsenal broke their six-year trophy drought. No-one stopped to consider little relegation-threatened Birmingham, whose own drought of major honours surpassed Arsenal's by 40 years.

The underdogs took the lead and dominated the game as Arsenal's easy cruise to silverware ground to a halt. Robin van Persie equalised soon after, but it was the Blues who seemed more up for the fight. A mix-up in defence between Laurent Koscielny and Wojciech Szczęsny in the final minute allowed a simple tap in for City striker Obafemi Martins.

The defeat left Arsenal's players in tatters on the pitch, but it was just reward for Birmingham who thoroughly deserved to take the trophy back to St Andrew's. Although watching Arsenal capitulate was enjoyable enough, it was heartening to see a club bereft of honours take a major domestic trophy for a change. It also showed that with hard work and determination, the form book can be overturned. Orient could continue dreaming.

```
 8.Oldham Athletic.....P33|W11|D13|L9 |F44|A45|46pts
 9.Rochdale...........P30|W11|D12|L7 |F42|A34|45pts
10.Colchester United...P32|W11|D12|L9 |F40|A42|45pts
11.Leyton Orient.......P30|W11|D11|L8 |F51|A42|44pts
12.Hartlepool United...P32|W12|D8 |L12|F33|A46|44pts
13.Carlisle United.....P31|W11|D9 |L11|F41|A35|42pts
14.Brentford..........P31|W12|D6 |L13|F37|A40|42pts
```

March 2011

<u>Wednesday 2nd March 2011</u>
<u>Arsenal v Orient</u>

Ten days on from the amazing night at Brisbane Road, the O's were off to the Emirates Stadium for the cup replay against Premier League opposition. The Orient message boards and Twitter were buzzing with excitement. Very few held out hopes of winning, but when a League One side gets the chance to visit Arsenal, one of the most successful club sides in England, winning the game hardly matters.

I was excited to be going to the Emirates, especially since I did not have the chance to visit Highbury before it was retired and turned into luxury apartments. Although it was the home of Tottenham's mortal enemy, I had to accept that the new stadium looked fantastic whenever I'd seen it on TV.

Before I could escape to north London for the match, I had to endure a monumentally boring day at work. With redundancy almost upon the department, there was so little for us to do in the office that I had taken to watching videos on YouTube, reliving glorious football moments I had witnessed from down the years.

With an hour to go, the monotony of the day was lifted when an announcement was made over the building's internal tannoy system. A suspect package had been discovered on Chancery Lane. Police and bomb disposal experts had advised us to leave via the back of the building. Everyone looked bemused and a little worried. Chancery Lane was at the heart of the legal district in the city, and it could be a target for terrorists or disgruntled convicts. The package, whatever it was, was eventually given the all-clear and the road reopened just in time for me to grab my coat and head up through Lincoln's Inn Fields to Holborn station.

Murph, Chas and Joss were waiting for me at the top of the escalators. With them were Danielle, Joss's wife Steph and his sister-in-law Georgina. Despite growing up in Bow, deep in the heartland of West Ham country, Georgina opted for a different claret and blue and was a devoted Aston Villa fan.

Fans from both teams packed into the carriages alongside exhausted office workers heading home. In fifteen minutes we arrived at Holloway Road station and made the short walk to the ground.

'You can always tell when there's a football match on,' I said as we walked down the dark backstreets towards the halo of light from the stadium shining over the roof tops. 'You can walk in the road and there are horses everywhere. Maybe this is what it was like a hundred years ago!'

The stadium looked impressive from the outside, lighting up a dark sky. Thousands of fans were milling about on the concourse or stood examining merchandise at the souvenir stalls. I bought a programme from one of the vendors.

'That's the first money I've ever given to Arsenal. I feel a bit grubby,' I said with a smile as I handed over the cash. 'How much of it goes to Orient?'

The vendor laughed and handed me my change. We followed the high, sweeping walls of the stadium round to the Drayton Park side to find the pub of the same name that Orient fans would gather in before kick-off. The pub was rammed tight with O's fans, so we went straight into the stadium. Negotiating my way through the automated turnstiles, almost tangling my bag in the revolving bars, I emerged into an open expanse of grey concrete. The only real colour other than a little red trim was a large sign fixed above the refreshments that simply declared 'Food + Drink'. After the grandness of the exterior, the concourse was a let down. It looked like a cross between a multi-storey car park and a food court at a shopping centre. It was the soulless underbelly of the stadium, more starkly exposed than at other newly-built stadia.

Having been to several new stadia, including the new Wembley, I wasn't surprised by the price of the food and beer. What made me laugh was the temerity of Arsenal's catering department, who marketed the £8.30 charge for a hot dog and beer as a 'deal'. The same thing costs a little over a fiver at Brisbane Road. The profiteering of clubs at the top of the game is something that needs addressing. If paying £50 for a game wasn't bad enough, ripping off your hungry and thirsty fans seems like adding insult to injury.

The experience felt very rushed and mechanical. There seemed to be very little heart or soul. How Arsenal fans put up with this week in week out I didn't know. Where was the love, the community spirit?

The space beneath the stand began to fill with Orient fans and a few familiar chants echoed around the walls. With ten minutes to go before kick-off, we went up a gangway to find our seats.

'Ah love this bit,' Joss said with a wistful smile on his face. 'Ah always get excited when ah'm walk'n up the stairs to get doon to the terraces'.

I agreed. We climbed a short flight of steps and emerged among the rows of Orient fans. The illuminated pitch was laid out before us like a flawless green carpet, skirting around it were curved tiers of seats. Walking out and viewing the pitch like that is perhaps as close as a fan can get to mirroring the players as they march from the tunnel onto the field to do battle.

Our seats were tucked in the corner of the lower tier to the right side of the goal. An overhang from the seats in the tier above us created a low ceiling, casting a shadow on the fans below and giving the impression that we were boxed in, but the view of the pitch and the other 9,000 travelling fans on the rows to our left and right was completely unobstructed.

Although the Orient fans had been fairly quiet before the game, intimidated perhaps by the grandeur of the surroundings, the noise level picked up and before long we were on our feet working our way through the full repertoire of songs. I paid £34 for my seat, and as it turned out, I never used it once.

The game began and settled quickly into a pattern. Arsenal held the ball in the Orient half, a persistent threat, Orient scraped hard for a sniff of possession. Arsenal opened the scoring within seven minutes when striker Marouane Chamakh found a bit of space in the penalty area and slotted the ball past Jamie Jones.

The goal did nothing to dampen the spirits of the away support. We continued our chorus of songs, drowning out the 40,000 home supporters who sat in virtual silence. The Brisbane Road match showed that at 1-0 there was always a chance of an unlikely comeback. Orient fashioned enough half chances and put together some nice passes on an immaculate playing surface to sow a seed of hope among the travelling support.

The result was put beyond doubt before half-time, however, when Niklas Bendtner, so profligate in the first match, bagged a quick-fire double. After netting his second, the Dane strode arrogantly over to the Orient support with his ear cupped, goading us into a response. He was on the receiving end of some serious stick at Brisbane Road, but a bit of perspective was needed. He should be scoring against us, we're in League One, so why the mocking?

'Niiiiklas Bendtner is a wanker, is a wanker, Niiiiklas Bendtner is a wanker, is a wanker!' was a fitting response. It made us feel better, but the score line on the huge scoreboard had a clear message. Arsenal 3, Leyton Orient 0. The cup run was over, Old Trafford would have to wait for another year. After squeaking past Dagenham and Redbridge, narrowly avoiding embarrassment at Droylsden, beating both Norwich and Swansea away from home, and most recently the bedlam of Téhoué's equaliser against the Gunners ten days ago, it was time for Orient to bow out of the FA Cup.

The second half was a procession for the home side. Bendtner rounded off a hat trick with a penalty on the hour and full-back Gael Clichy crashed in a decent effort from outside the box to make it 5-0. The home fans remained unmoved. No noise, no songs and with fifteen minutes to go, they began to file out of the stadium.

'Is there a fire drill?' we sang as the supporters disappeared into the night.

'Worst fans in London!' I shouted, and a huge section of the O's fans took up the chant, pointing across at the departing home fans in derision. Feeling quite pleased with myself, I glanced at Murph and Chas who were looking at me indignantly.

'Bit harsh,' Chas said.

'You're O's boys now, and let's face it,' I said, pointing across the pitch at the empty seats, 'that is embarrassing!'

With just a minute to go Orient had one last chance to salvage a bit of pride, but Dean Cox's effort went agonisingly wide. At the final whistle the players trooped over to thank us for our support and we showed them our appreciation for a fantastic cup run.

We left the ground and followed the crowds onto Holloway Road and down towards the top of Upper Street, the Orient fans still singing all the way. A sign offering a car wash for £5 hung above a deserted car park.

'Look at that!' I said, pointing at the sign. 'Having your car washed by hand is half the price of buying a hot dog at the Emirates. There's something fundamentally wrong with that!'

Saturday 5th March 2011
Orient v Notts County

Back to reality. Winning the cup was always nothing more than the stuff of dreams, but a play-off place was a realistic target and and three points on Saturday were vital to that cause.

Notts County, under the stewardship of former England captain Paul Ince, were struggling for form and hovering above the relegation zone, albeit with a comfortable points cushion from the teams below. Orient, on the other hand, were looking to extend their unbeaten league run to eleven. Their last defeat was the New Year's Day drubbing at the hands of Brighton.

I arrived at the Supporters Club in time for the early kick-off Premier League derby between Birmingham and West Brom. It was Beer Festival Day, barrels of real ale were stacked up by the far wall and a makeshift bar had been set out with trestle tables. I don't usually partake in ale, preferring the uncouth fizz of a premium lager, but £2.50 for a pint seemed like a good reason to try some.

Chas had been out the previous evening, celebrating the last day of his job before moving on to pastures new, and he turned up looking the worse for wear an hour before kick-off. I was still in employment limbo. I had not heard about the job I had interviewed for and there was no definitive news on my current job either, although surely the writing was on the wall on that front. Jamie had been skiing in Bulgaria so missed the trip to the Emirates in the week and was making another late dash from the airport to get to the game.

It was good to be back in the familiar and welcoming surroundings of Brisbane Road after the soulless, corporate experience at the Emirates. Once again it was freezing cold and everyone was wrapped up tightly against the bitter chill. I was already looking forward to some warmer games in April.

Orient started positively. There was a sense of belief and confidence about the players as they knocked it around neatly, and that belief was rubbing off on us in the stands. With just eight minutes gone, little Tom Carroll, who had broken into the starting line-up recently, justified his inclusion with a perfect chipped through ball to Cox. The winger dashed into the box, waited for the keeper to go to ground, and clipped the ball over him and into the net.

Orient dominated the rest of the half without adding to the score and continued to run the game after the interval. Tom Carroll provided the key to another move that should have led to a second goal, finding Alex Revell with another superb through ball. The big striker scampered towards goal, rounded the keeper and rolled the ball towards the unguarded net. It looked to be a certain goal, but a defender slid from out of nowhere to clear the ball. The crowd at the far end erupted in protest and Revell gesticulated wildly at the referee, pointing to his arm. The ref agreed that the defender handled the ball and pointed to the penalty spot.

Paul Ince did not agree. He kicked off a scuffle on the touchline, shouting angrily at Russell Slade and pushing and shoving in front of the dug-outs. We had no idea what had gone on, but whatever it was it was enough to make mild-mannered Slade uncharacteristically angry. The referee marched over to discuss matters with his assistant and restore order on the touchline. After a long chat with his colleague, he dispatched an incensed Paul Ince to the stands.

With usual penalty taker Ben Chorley out through injury, the responsibility fell to Revell. He was forced to stand alone on the penalty spot with the ball under his arm, the pressure slowly building on him, while the referee settled down the commotion on the sideline. There was a distinct feeling around us in the stand that Revell would miss the spot kick. Too much time had elapsed and he was in danger of over-thinking the penalty. We were proved right and his tame kick was easily saved.

Sensing this was their moment to get back in the game, County pushed forward. Orient, despite looking comfortable for most of the game, were now on the back foot.

During a brief lull in the action, my eyes were drawn away from the pitch just in time to see a man in the West Stand go flying through the air as he tripped descending the stairs, bouncing down to pitch level, ten feet from where he had begun his flight. Some others noticed this random moment and cheered mockingly at what looked like a nasty fall. Stewards dashed to the stricken man's aid, picked him up and led him to an empty seat. He looked dazed and in shock but was still walking and in one piece. As he was led away he received another big cheer from the crowd and an unsympathetic chorus of 'she fell over' for good measure.

Back on the pitch, Orient weathered the Notts County storm and were looking for a killer goal. It came with ten minutes left. Cox swung in a free kick from the left hand side and right-back Andrew Whing kept a diving header low past the keeper to make the points safe.

The Beer Festival in the Supporters Club was in full swing a few minutes after the final whistle, helped no doubt by dropping the price to £1.50 a pint. With Orient now up to ninth in the table, there was plenty to celebrate. Jamie left almost immediately after the final whistle to enjoy courtside tickets at a basketball game that were supposed to be worth £1000.

'You not gonna stay and have a few £1.50 pints to celebrate?' I said as he pulled his jacket on.

'No, the game starts at seven and I want to have a couple of freebie beers beforehand,' Jamie said.

'A grand just to watch a load of lanky blokes play netball? Where'd you get that type of money from?' Murph asked mockingly.

'You think I'm paying for it? No chance! Corporate seats mate. Going to take full advantage,' he said, bidding us goodbye.

Orient travelled to the West Midlands on Tuesday night to face Walsall, hoping to further extend their unbeaten league run. Eleven matches without a loss became twelve when they returned after a relatively trouble-free 2-0 win. The O's were striding up the league, and with every game they seemed to be growing in confidence. There were more than enough games left in the season to climb into promotion contention, unthinkable given the horrific start to the season.

The same evening, Arsenal were played off the park by Barcelona in the Champions League. They threw away a 2-1 lead from the first leg to lose 4-3 on aggregate. The Gunners had spent long periods of the tie ahead on aggregate, but in reality there was a huge gulf in quality. Niklas Bendtner presumably didn't bother mocking the Barca fans.

As Spurs were scheduled to play the following evening, I resisted the urge to send Murph and Chas a message basking in the enjoyment of Arsenal's early exit from the competition. I'd supported Spurs long enough to know they were capable of making me eat my words. They were hosting AC Milan at White Hart Lane, hoping to hold onto the slender 1-0 lead they earned at the San Siro.

I was nervous about the game all day, and it got worse as we approached kick-off. I considered avoiding the game altogether to save myself from the stress, but I simply had to watch Spurs in the knockout stages of the Champions League at White Hart Lane. I met Neil, the Sheffield Wednesday fan, at the Water Poet to watch the match on TV. It was a good job he was there as he helped keep me sane throughout the ninety minutes that followed. Ninety agonising minutes.

White Hart Lane was in full voice, but the game was cagey and there were few chances. The longer it continued at 0-0, the more I thought Spurs would do something daft and throw it away. Yet they kept at it with cool heads and looked resolute in defence, epitomised by an acrobatic clearance by William Gallas off the Spurs goal line to prevent a Milan breakthrough.

I got talking with another fretful-looking Spurs fan. He couldn't resist the urge and had sent gloating messages to his Arsenal mates the night before.

'You really should have waited until we were through,' I said to him.

'I know. I'm regretting it now. I'm so fucking nervous!' he replied anxiously, rocking on his heels and with his arms crossed tight across his chest. If Spurs lost, he had made his own humiliation that little bit worse by sending those texts.

The fourth official lifted a board, announcing three minutes of stoppage time. Even Neil looked nervous. In the least dramatic end to one of the biggest matches ever hosted at the Lane, the ball trickled out for a throw in near the halfway line and it was all over. My new Spurs companion and I jumped around in delight along with a number of other Spurs fans who had endured the torment with us. Spurs were through to the Champions League quarter-finals.

Tuesday: Orient win and Arsenal lose. Wednesday: Spurs win. Thursday: new job.

I was called to meet a woman from Human Resources and the director of Product Development in the company I work for. They were both smiling.

'Well Adam, we'll get right to the point. We aren't able to offer you the role I'm afraid.' My heart sank. 'But we do have an offer for you.' I listened on. 'We really liked your presentation and you did a great interview. The only reason we can't take you on is because you lack experience. So we'd like to offer you a secondment into the department for six months to get some experience. How does that sound?'

It sounds fucking superb to me, I felt like saying. Instead I politely thanked them and said I'd be delighted.

The relief I felt walking out of the meeting room was like a weight being lifted from my shoulders. The prospect of unemployment that had been hanging over me had been raised, for another six months at least. Who knows, maybe they would keep me on at the end of it.

Back in my department, the news was less positive. Human resources were there too with a stack of ominous white envelopes. Our jobs were being made redundant. My manager looked thoroughly pissed off and a colleague of mine, usually so calm, was choking back rage as he gave the management his opinions on the whole situation. He did well not to lose his rag completely.

We were given the afternoon off to reflect on the big news and decided to spend it in the Knights Templar pub. Redundancy and job offer in the same day. That had to be some kind of record.

Saturday 12th March 2011
Orient v Oldham Athletic

Spring arrived at last. The skies were clear and for the first time in months I was confident I wouldn't get frostbite at Brisbane Road. Unfortunately, the tube network is as unreliable as any weather forecast and the Central Line was closed again, meaning I had to get a train to Stratford and walk the rest of the way. In the carriage I overheard two West Ham fans joking about Orient's precarious future over the Olympic Stadium debacle. A surge of fury built up inside me but I restrained myself from interjecting and allowed them to wallow in ignorance.

The FA Cup quarter-final between Bolton and newly-crowned League Cup champions Birmingham was on the TV in the Supporters Club. Both FA and League cups have suffered over the last decade as European competitions have outshone them and clubs have focused their efforts on league performances. Some believe the romance of getting to Wembley has gone, but after Orient's exciting and engaging cup run, it seemed to me that reports of the FA Cup's demise were greatly exaggerated. Judging by the 3-2 ding-dong Bolton and Birmingham fixture, they clearly hadn't lost the love for the cup either.

Animated chatter broke out among the usually unexcitable veteran supporters as a besuited, grey-haired man, who looked to be in his mid-fifties, strolled through the doors and shook a few hands.

'Who's that?' I asked at the bar.

'That's Peter Kitchen,' the barman said. 'He's a legend around here!'

The reverence with which this former player was held by the fans implied that it was the equivalent of Gary Mabbutt walking through the doors at the Bell and Hare in Tottenham. I made a mental note to learn a bit more about Orient's past. If I was to continue my journey as an O's fan properly, I should know where the club came from. Being able to talk knowledgeably about a club's past is as important as predicting its future.

With the future in mind, Murph had been speaking with Tim who worked behind the bar about potential ways to raise the club's profile. Murph was no marketing guru, but he is an enthusiastic and creative type and Tim seemed grateful for the input.

'There must be thousands of blokes in London who aren't originally from around here and support other clubs but fancy going along to watch some footy at weekends,' Murph said. 'Do a bit of advertising over at Canary Wharf or something, I reckon it would pull in loads of punters.'

'It'd be good to have at least the club badge on a sign down at the tube station,' I added. 'Other clubs do it so it can't be too hard to organise.'

'Why don't you write to the club's Chief Exec?' Tim suggested. 'He's always keen to have input from the fans. He'll listen to your ideas.'

Up in the stands, we debated the potential outcome of the match. Oldham were on a bad run, having failed to win their last eight games. Orient, on the other hand, were rampant. In theory it should be a comfortable win, but undefeated streaks have a habit of coming to an abrupt end at unexpected hands.

As it was, the match stayed true to the form book. Orient dominated the first half without finding the all-important breakthrough. Tom Carroll was at the centre of things, knocking the ball around calmly and precisely. At just seventeen years of age, his future in football was looking extremely bright. A new face occupied the centre-back spot vacated by the injured Ben Chorley. Adam Barrett, a bald-headed beast of a man who had been on Orient's books as a youngster, had been brought in on loan from Crystal Palace. His giant frame filled the Chorley-sized gap admirably in the first 45 minutes.

The second half was much scrappier. The visitors were given a lot of leeway by the referee as persistent fouls and time-wasting went unpunished. Orient lost their rhythm, and as the game wore on, 0-0 started to look more and more likely. Slade turned to his substitutes for an answer. Paul-Jose M'Poku entered the game and his skill immediately opened things up.

With the clock approaching ninety minutes, M'Poku picked the ball up deep on the left hand side. Thirty yards from goal, he looked up and hit a perfect drive, swinging his boot cleanly through the ball, sending it rocketing towards us in the Tommy Johnston Stand. We had a great perspective of the slight swerve as it beat the outstretched arm of Oldham's Man United loanee Ben Amos and hit the back of the net with a satisfying crack of nylon. It was a goal worthy of winning any game. Although the goalkeeper had little chance of stopping it, a chant of 'you'll never play for Man U!' filled the Tommy Johnston Stand.

The final whistle confirmed another three points for the O's. I started singing. 'We're going up, we're going up, the O's are going up!'

I felt a tap on my shoulder and Paul from the seats behind us shook his head with a disapproving expression on his face. 'Hold on,' he wisely declared. 'Let's not get carried away.'

I laughed and shrugged my shoulders, but stopped my over-confident proclamation. Clearly I was in danger of jinxing us. Where this positivity came from I didn't know. I would never have dared say such a thing if Spurs were in the same situation. I had learned it was wiser to expect the worst but hope for the best when it came to Tottenham. Orient were yet to disappoint me in the same way Spurs had done over the years. With Orient, I was yet to learn that lesson.

We stayed in the Supporters Club to watch Man United play Arsenal in the FA Cup, imagining wistfully what might have been. Our vanquishers became the vanquished as United ran out 2-0 victors. No doubt the rest of the country were happy to watch the big two in action, but I would have given anything for Orient to have been there.

On the bus back to Stratford, we got talking to an Orient fan who lived in Brighton. He travelled up at least ten times a season to see the O's play. As we spoke, the bus rattled past the Olympic Park. The shadow of the new stadium reminded me that Orient would need many committed fans like this chap in the coming years.

Orient travelled to Hartlepool on Tuesday night. The journey is a 500-mile round trip and even on a Saturday the match would have only attracted a smattering of hardy travellers. I've always had a lot of respect for fans who make epic journeys like this to watch their team, although I also question their sanity.

There was no possibility of us making the trip, which meant the usual routine of sitting with the laptop and refreshing the screen every two minutes. Radio, however, came to the rescue. Murph found out that the match was being broadcast live on Radio London 94.9. Within an hour the word had spread far and wide on Twitter and hundreds of happy O's fans were listening to the action at Victoria Park.

In the age of the smartphone and satellite TV, the value of radio in football is often underestimated. A familiar-but-dying sight on the terraces is that of fans clutching pocket radios and listening intently to the scores as they come in up and down the country, speakers pressed tightly to their ears. I had been one of those fans. I was a proud owner of a small, grey pocket radio and as a teenager it was my constant companion at every game, whether at White Hart Lane or non-league Billericay Town.

Radio commentators are amongst the most gifted of their craft. Their challenge is to paint an ever-changing picture of the action without pausing for thought. The rhythm, pitch and speed of the commentary are tuned perfectly to the tempo of the game.

Listening to the Hartlepool match was as raw an experience as it could possibly have been. The background noise was so clear that the commentators seemed to be sat right in the middle of the crowd. Orient dominated possession and the commentators were certain that they were on top. As good as we were playing, having no awareness of where the ball was made me anxious. Having a virtual blindfold applied whilst trying to follow a match makes radio-football an agonisingly tense affair. When in reality an opposition player's shot has gone so far over the bar it has cleared the stand, in your mind it was inches from goal and the keeper had no chance of saving it.

Just before the half hour, the commentary team were sent into raptures when Jimmy Smith hit a superb volley from a Dean Cox cross to put the visitors ahead. The admiring reviews of Orient's play continued as the half wore on. They were in complete control and playing some beautiful football. It was a pity I couldn't witness it with my own eyes, but I felt a little pride as the match reporters piled on the praise.

The technicians seemed to forget to switch the microphones off at half-time and the conversation between the commentators was clearly audible. The O's were, according to the reporters, looking cocky. It was a sneeringly negative appraisal in stark contrast to the acclaim Orient's play had received live on air moments earlier. It left me wondering what other things were said when the microphones were switched off and whether they always eulogise the team on air.

The second half seemed to be very different to the first. Orient were squandering possession readily and Hartlepool were pressing for an equaliser. Either that, or I had learned to take some of the commentators' observations with a pinch of salt and was trying to second-guess what they really meant.

It was clear that Hartlepool were battering Orient's defence, but their shots were stopped either by Jamie Jones or the woodwork. The frustration of the home crowd was easily discernable from around the commentators as several earthy north-eastern voices turned the airwaves blue. It was an agonising wait as the 90-minute mark approached, but Orient hung on and achieved a record of fourteen games unbeaten in the league.

The push for a play-off place was well and truly on. If they really were as good as the Radio London commentary team suggested in the first half, who knows, maybe automatic promotion wasn't out of the question?

The following weekend, Orient popped across London to Brentford. I passed on the trip, choosing instead to take up the offer of a ticket at White Hart Lane courtesy of my Spurs-supporting mate Andy. Having not been to the Lane all season and with Spurs taking a back seat to my time at Orient, I felt I owed it to my old club to go along at least once, just to remind them I was still around. They were probably missing me. And since Spurs were playing against West Ham, I could justify the trip by hoping they could thrash a common enemy.

Stopping to top up my Oyster card for the week ahead, I walked back out of the station. Somewhere between the ticket machine and leaving the station some degenerate piece of pond life reached his or her grubby paw into my rucksack and pinched my wallet. I didn't realise it had gone until I saw the gaping maw of my rucksack front pocket flapping open.

I'd lived in London for almost five years and this was the first time I had been a victim of any sort of crime, not a bad record for someone dwelling in one of the world's largest metropolises, but I felt violated and was spitting mad about it.

Once I'd calmed down, I cancelled my bank card which was fortunately the only thing of value in the wallet. On checking my bank account the following day, I saw that not only had the perpetrator withdrawn £40 from my account, they'd paid for a tube ticket at St Paul's. They must have been peering over my shoulder at the ticket machine and then lifted the wallet from the pocket of my bag as I exited the station. Thankfully it was before pay day and my account was as empty as ever, which restricted their chance to pounce on much money. A small victory for my big-spending lifestyle.

The game had been shifted to a lunchtime kick-off, so I met Andy at Liverpool Street at 11am and we hopped on the train up to Northumberland Park. At least I had plenty of credit on my Oyster card.

'You know, I haven't seen Spurs lose at White Hart Lane for over ten years,' I said as the train rattled its way up past Stamford Hill, 'although the last two games I've seen have been 0-0.'

Andy contemplated my record. 'I don't know whether to be glad you're coming or whether we're doomed to another bore draw.'

We enjoyed some pre-match pints at the Olive Branch on Park Lane and met friends of his who were planning a jaunt to Madrid to watch Spurs take on Real Madrid in the Champions League quarter-finals. I thought about the commitment they had to Spurs and wondered whether I'd been too hasty to give it all up. I was enjoying pints and talking football much the same as I did at Orient, and although these weren't close friends, they were good company. Maybe watching Spurs could prove to be the same experience as watching Orient?

My decision to take up the Orient season ticket was vindicated once we got to the ground.

'Right,' Andy said, offering his hand in farewell. 'We're sat up in the Park Lane. Meet you back here after the game?'

'Yeah, no probs,' I said reluctantly, and turned away to the East Stand to find my seat. I was on my own. I would have none of the camaraderie, none of the banter and I would be surrounded by unfamiliar people.

The game was a good one, as Spurs-West Ham games often are. I enjoyed it of course, I always enjoy watching Spurs live, but the experiences I'd had at Brisbane Road was so different to this. The crowd was louder, the stadium bigger, the play quicker and more skilful – but the same empty feeling I experienced in the past was still there. There was a distance, not necessarily between myself and the team on the pitch, or even between myself and the fans around me, but between myself and the club.

Spurs were battering their opponents but could not find the net. Hammers captain Scott Parker was in superb form, shielding his back four from the onslaught as a midfield anchor, and Robert Green, the much maligned fall guy of England's World Cup opener against the USA, was looking unbeatable in goal. The full-time whistle blew. West Ham had nicked an unlikely point in a no-score draw.

I made my way down through the stairways to meet Andy at the corner of the ground. He was smiling but shaking his head. 'I knew it. You jinxed it!' he said.

'Still maintains my unbeaten record though,' I replied.

'If that's the case, maybe we should get you a ticket every week.'

'Can't mate, got Orient to go to now.'

We headed back to Bishopsgate and into the Water Poet. Orient were losing 2-0 to Brentford. The unbeaten run was under threat. I continued to check the scores as I finished my drink and started to head home. Scott McGleish pulled one back, but time was ticking by. With a saveloy and chips bundled up tightly in newspaper, I walked down Hanbury Street and I phoned Murph. His excited voice answered.

'Alright mate,' I said, 'is it still 2-1?'

'For God's sake! I thought you were calling to say we'd equalised!' he groaned in frustration.

'Sorry, was just checking in.'

'Shit,' he said dejectedly, 'it's just flashed up that it's over. 2-1. Fucking Brentford.'

The statistical record was over, but it was vital at this stage in the season Orient didn't lose their heads. Another London derby against Dagenham and Redbridge was up next, and I remembered all too well how the reverse fixture had turned out back in September.

In the meantime, I had a new job to start on Monday. I didn't know what to be more nervous about, the new role or the Daggers visiting Brisbane Road.

<u>Tuesday 22nd March 2011</u>
<u>Orient v Dagenham and Redbridge</u>

The first day of my job went well. There was a lot to learn, but I had the benefit of knowing most of my new colleagues from the past four-and-a-half years. I felt energised and revitalised, a far cry from the bottomless pit I stared into a few weeks before.

I bounced out of the office that Tuesday evening and shot straight over to Brisbane Road. I had ditched the casual attire of my previous department for a more professional get-up; shiny black shoes, a crisp TM Lewin shirt and a pair of grey pin-stripe trousers. It didn't go unnoticed with the boys.

'Blimey Ad,' Jamie exclaimed, 'I can't remember the last time I saw you so smart. Have you got a proper job now?'

'I do indeed,' I said proudly, and began to fill in the details of what my new role involved.

'Anyone want a drink?' Chas asked.

'Can you just get me an empty pint glass?' I replied.

He returned with an empty glass, looking puzzled. I reached into my bag, and looking around guiltily, pulled out a can of Strongbow. My new-found professionalism was dispelled by a lack of cash. My new bank card was still in the post, so I had to scrape a few coins together and buy four cans of Strongbow from the supermarket on the way to the game.

'You pikey!' Jamie exclaimed with incredulity.

Protesting his jibe, I explained my financial situation.

'Goes to show you,' Murph said after I had finished, 'you can dress him up in new clothes and polish his shoes but underneath he's still the same old Ad.'

The match was what I fully expected from a Daggers fixture. Their hoof-it-long football that caused Orient such problems at the start of the season was having the same debilitating effect. Orient couldn't find their rhythm and the Dagenham defence was comfortable dealing with any high balls the O's were forced to hoist into the box.

The visitors stole the lead after eleven minutes, some calamitous goalkeeping from Jones providing the break-through. The goal caused moans and groans from the home crowd, probably from frustration at Jones' error, but I had a sneaking suspicion that it was also from knowing full well we had 80 minutes more of this turgid display to endure.

The doom and gloom had descended again. After going unbeaten for fourteen games and rising meteorically up the league, Saturday's defeat had knocked the belief out of the supporters. Now, a goal behind to relegation-fodder Dagenham, the crowd all but gave up any hope. They had seen it all before.

The second half was as dire as the first, with sloppy passing and incoherent, disjointed movement. Dagenham and Redbridge were squeezing the life out of their opponents like a giant snake. Russell Slade, as he had done to good effect before, threw M'Poku on to spark some life into the side. It didn't feel like a game for his trickery, and he was more likely to drift into anonymity as Dagenham's cloggers thundered remorselessly into challenges.

How wrong I was. The little midfielder picked out the ball and danced into the box with minutes remaining, only to be felled by a lunging tackle before he could pull the trigger. The crowd leapt to their feet in delight as the referee pointed straight to the penalty spot and then brandished a red card to the guilty defender. In his excitement M'Poku made to place the ball on the spot to take the kick himself, but McGleish pulled rank and pushed him away, placed the ball purposefully on its mark and stepped back.

The home crowd was tense and quiet; the Daggers fans were waving and whistling, attempting to put the Orient striker off as best as they could. We waited for the whistle.

McGleish strode forward and sent the keeper the wrong way, placing the ball perfectly into the corner of the goal. Brisbane Road erupted in joy and relief as the veteran wheeled away to celebrate in the corner.

Orient had an excellent chance to grab all three points almost immediately after the kick-off, but it went begging. The board was raised signifying five minutes of stoppage time. Could they nick it after such an awful performance?

The final whistle blew and the contrast between the fans was evident. The Orient fans rose in relieved applause, happy to have nicked a point. The away fans roared in celebration as if they had won the league, the point a valuable addition to their relegation-threatened tally. Chants of 'going down, going down, going down' were directed at them from the Orient fans, reminding them of the reality of their league position. They replied with 'I want to go home, I want to go hoooome, Leyton's a shithole, I want to go home!'

'Who are they kidding?' a bloke in front of us laughed. 'I've been to Dagenham. I'd have thought they'd be thankful for a night away from the place!'

Saturday 26th March 2011
Orient v Yeovil Town

With Chas and Murph's birthdays coming up, the visit of Yeovil became the springboard for birthday celebrations and a night out in Wanstead. Our friends Alexi and Worz travelled to Leyton from Milton Keynes and West

Bromwich to join us and took the vacant places of the absent Jamie, in Dublin again, and Joss, who had gone to see family in Durham. To get in the celebratory spirit, we decided to honour Russell Slade, Orient's follicly-challenged manager, by donning bald wigs and Orient baseball caps.

The match was brought forward to 1 o'clock owing to England's European Championship qualifying match versus Wales, which kicked off at 3. Scotland were playing Brazil in an international friendly at the Emirates the following day, and there were several groups of kilted men making their way to Brisbane Road, taking the opportunity to enjoy an Orient game while they were in town. With men in skirts walking through east London it was unlikely anyone would blink twice at us in our bald wigs and caps. At least the Scots were dressed for the climate. It was a fresh spring afternoon with clear skies, and the tight rubber bald caps we were wearing caused sweat to run down into our faces.

Orient started well. After the claustrophobia of the Dagenham and Redbridge match, this time they looked to play some expansive football. Perhaps they got a little too ambitious with their passes though, because a poor clearance fell to Yeovil's Shaun MacDonald about 30 yards from goal. He controlled the wayward pass, set himself and unleashed a bullet of a shot that pinged off the upright and into the net, leaving Jamie Jones stood like a statue. The few fans that had made the long trip to London from the south-west exploded with noise. It was as good a goal as any that I'd seen at Brisbane Road, or at any ground ever for that matter, and it seemed to knock the stuffing out of the Orient players.

With Alex Revell out injured, Jonathan Téhoué, the hero of the Arsenal game, was making a rare start. He strolled around aimlessly and casually, much to the crowd's chagrin. He could strike a ball as cleanly as anyone I'd seen but he lacked the industry of his injured teammate and was already proving to be a marginal player in this game.

A goal down, Orient suffered another blow. Matt Spring, not the quickest of players, made a rash challenge on the halfway line. It was late and warranted no more than a yellow card, but the referee showed him red. The home fans were incensed and the ref came in for some hammering.

Yeovil, now both a goal and a man to the good, turned the screw. Shaun MacDonald turned in a second goal from a close but narrow angle. The crowd felt the game was as good as over already, but little were we to know the full extent.

The referee, having wrongly sent Spring off, was losing the plot. He missed several clear free kicks for both sides and an obvious elbow in the face to Scott McGleish that should have resulted in another sending off. He then confounded our anger by awarding Yeovil a penalty after judging that Dawson handled the ball in the box, when it actually hit the Orient captain in the face a good foot outside the penalty area. The linesman, who was staring straight at the incident with a clear view, didn't signal anything. The ref, stood twenty feet away, overruled him.

'This is unbelievable!' Murph shouted.

'What the fuck is the matter with that prick?' Chas added.

An inevitable chorus of 'the referee's a wanker' echoed round the stands, and once the penalty was scored, was followed by 'three-nil to the referee, three-nil to the referee!'

'Ref! You've ruined my day!' I yelled. A burly looking supporter a few rows in front turned round and shouted 'well said!' in agreement.

At half-time we retired to the refuge of the bar. As we walked down the steps I overheard a young boy speaking to his dad.

'Dad what's a wonker?'

'It's a rude word, and it's not wonker, it's wanker. But I don't want to hear you saying it, OK?'

You would have forgiven the troubled father allowing his young offspring the freedom to say what he liked after that refereeing display. The worst I had ever seen by some distance. What a wonker.

In the bar we were quick to scapegoat our two guests, Worz and Alexi, as the jinxes who had brought the referee and scoreline upon us like a curse from their heathen villages in the north.

While I was at the bar two coppers made their way through the crowd. One guy stopped them.

'Excuse me officers, I think you need to get over to the changing rooms, there's a guy in there guilty of impersonating a referee.'

Everyone within ear shot laughed, including the coppers, one of whom replied, 'I'm not sure we can do anything about that. Maybe we can get him for daylight robbery?'

Moments into the second half, Yeovil made it 4-0. 'For fuck's sake,' I said as we sat down. 'We should have stayed in the bar.'

Knowing full well whose fault it was, the crowd refused to criticise the team and kept on singing. The players were endeavouring to get back into a game that was well and truly lost. Their efforts were rewarded with a consolation goal scored by Cox, whose shot deflected off a defender and into the net.

'We're gonna win 5-4, we're gonna win 5-4, we're gonna win 5-4!' we sang in celebration. Gallows humour is a staple requirement for all football fans.

The referee continued to bungle his way through the game and the Yeovil fans over to our left were strangely muted for a side winning 4-1 away from home, as though even they realised they had twelve men on the field.

The one-man advantage was exposed again before the end. Orient were caught out at the back and the visitors made it 5-1, but it meant very little in the grand scheme of things. The cheers of the away fans at full-time were drowned out with fresh abuse directed towards the referee, who was escorted from the field by a couple of policemen.

Perhaps they were the same ones from the bar arresting him on daylight robbery charges.

Back in the Supporters Club, the atmosphere was subdued. No-one seemed that interested in the England-Wales match, despite the Three Lions taking an early 2-0 lead. Orient were looking less likely to secure a play-off berth after taking only one point from the last three matches, although many other teams in the hunt were also dropping points. A few nay-sayers in the Supporters Club were claiming that the referee had ruined our entire season, although I remained more positive.

Although it was ill-timed, the Yeovil result was just a minor blip. Momentum is everything in the play-offs, it often the team that finishes the lowest of the qualifying teams that wins the play-off final – they squeeze into the play-offs on the back of a great run and continue that form in the knock-out stages. Blackpool, Crystal Palace and Burnley had all done it from the Championship in recent years, and I was hopeful we could be that team in League One. With nine matches to go, there was plenty of time for Orient to pick up momentum again.

Outside, the Yeovil team coach was filling up with departing players. 'Is the ref getting on with you?' one guy shouted, and this was followed by some abuse aimed at the players themselves. As the coach pulled away, three play-ers lined up against the windows and held up five fingers on one hand, one on the other. It was a fair comeback and drew a few accepting laughs from the watching Orient fans. If you give it, you have to learn to take it: another lesson all football fans must learn and learn quickly.

```
 4.Southampton.........P36|W19|D8 |L9 |F65|A31|65pts
 5.MK Dons.............P39|W19|D8 |L12|F56|A49|65pts
 6.Bournemouth.........P38|W17|D11|L10|F62|A41|62pts
 7.Leyton Orient.......P37|W15|D12|L10|F60|A50|57pts
 8.Rochdale............P37|W15|D12|L10|F50|A41|57pts
 9.Brentford...........P39|W16|D7 |L16|F46|A49|55pts
10.Colchester United...P39|W14|D12|L13|F48|A50|54pts
```

April 2011

Eight months seemed to have passed in the blink of an eye and there was just a handful of pages left in my season ticket. Spring is the time of the football harvest – the wheat and the chaff are separated, some doomed to relegation, others moving onwards and upwards to better things. Brighton had all but confirmed automatic promotion, but who accompanied them to the Championship was still far from decided. Orient were firmly cemented in the pack of play-off chasers. The rollercoaster we had been aboard since August was showing no signs of slowing down.

It was Stacey's birthday on the last day of March. Unlike me, Stace did not want to spend her birthday at a football match, so accompanying Murph to the Valley to watch Orient take on Charlton the weekend after would have been less a 'spare room offence' and more 'castration by butter knife'. As I wanted to keep the contents of my trousers in one piece, I opted to take Stace out around town for the afternoon. The O's were beaten 3-1 in southeast London and a furious Murph and weary-looking Danielle met us in the Golden Heart on Commercial Street that evening.

'I just don't get it,' he blustered as we leaned against the bar waiting for our drinks. 'Why do we always get the terrible refs? I can't remember one this season who had a decent game. We had a perfectly good goal ruled out when it was 1-1, and we were on top at the time.'

After watching the BBC's *Football League Show* that evening, I decided that Murph had a point. Premier League managers are often sounding off in the press about poor officiating when a decision goes against them and the debate rages for days. I sympathise somewhat with Premier League refs. The game is played at such pace, in front of an audience of millions and for such high stakes that, under such scrutiny, it is almost impossible to be right. The standard of refereeing in League One has no such mitigations. A season of bearing the brunt of such decisions had confirmed that poor officiating is part of the game in League One. Alex Ferguson and Arsene Wenger should count themselves lucky.

If refereeing blunders weren't bad enough, the defeat to Charlton allowed Rochdale to leapfrog us in the table. With at least two of the play-off places virtually decided, the final two positions were going to be fought over tooth and nail. Did Orient have the stomach for such a fight?

<u>Tuesday 5th April 2011</u>
<u>Orient v Plymouth Argyle</u>

To the general incredulity of those that knew me, Tottenham's Champions League quarter-final against Real Madrid, the biggest game in the club's recent history, took a back seat to League One. Orient were up against Plymouth in a rearranged fixture from frozen December. As much as I wanted to see the Spurs game, it made no sense to sit in a pub watching a game and swearing at a TV screen when I had a ticket to a different match where my voice would be heard. It didn't seem to make any sense to any of my Spurs-supporting mates, but it seemed perfectly logical to me.

Although I couldn't watch both matches, it didn't stop me worrying and fretting about both all day. Four-hour meetings are not the best preparation for two enormous football matches. For Orient, a win would propel them back into seventh after five games without a win, gaining ground on stuttering Bournemouth in sixth. For Spurs, any kind of result in Madrid would be magnificent. My stomach was in knots and I was desperate to escape the confines of the office for the sanctity of the Supporters Club.

At 5:30 I shot out of the door and into the bustle of rush hour on the Central Line. In my haste I left my Orient scarf hanging on the coat stand. It was a bad omen, one that my already-scrambled nerves could do without. I cursed my stupidity and wallowed in guilt for the fact I'd probably just jinxed Orient to humiliation and defeat. I didn't notice Joss stood waiting outside the station, and it took a good nudge in my ribs to snap me out of my trance.

In the Supporters Club, Murph arrived with some surprising news. 'I'm quitting my job,' he said matter-of-factly. For the past year, he had been working for the London Olympics as Football Venue Results Manager. His role was to organise and implement the systems and processes that went in to tracking all the football statistics at the forthcoming Olympic Games. The job had taken him up and down the country viewing the biggest stadia from Old Trafford to Wembley.

'What? Why?' I said, goggling in astonishment, 'I thought you loved that job?'

'I've had enough of the bullshit. I had to deal with all sorts of internal and external politics and you know what I'm like. If I think someone's a prick, I'll tell them. I don't think it made me too popular.'

'Who tipped the balance in the end, FIFA or the FA?'

'Bit of both really, and it wasn't just them. I was being asked – no, forced – to bend over backwards to please them and I just couldn't do it. They've been a ballache from the start and I've had enough of it.'

'But it paid so well, and you've got the wedding in a few months. What are you going to do for work?'

'I'm handing in my notice in August before I go on honeymoon and then I'm going into business on my own.'

'Doing what?'

'I'm starting my own clothing label.'

My jaw dropped for a second time. Murph was not one for fashion or creativity, so this was about the last thing I expected him to say. 'What in God's name makes you want to do that?'

'Well, I figured there are plenty of labels out there that sit comfortably in the middle of the road making decent money, and I thought, why can't I do that?'

I had to admire his ambition, although his choice of profession was about as random as it got. Amid all of this, and to add to the bizarre course the conversation had taken, Jamie had arrived and was suffering a bad case of the shits.

'Oooh,' he groaned, clutching his stomach as if another movement was imminent. 'This is such bad timing, I've got the Paris marathon on Sunday.'

'If your legs are running as fast as your bowels are you should do fine!'

Our pre-match prattle and a couple of pints did wonders to settle my nervous stomach (the less said about Jamie's the better) but the butterflies returned as we took our seats for the start of the game. The midweek atmosphere was as subdued as ever. Saturday crowds have the benefit of a good night's sleep and a few hours to tank themselves up. After a busy day at work, Tuesday night fixtures are used as a welcome intermission from the nine-to-five rather than the all-day knees-up that the weekend offers.

Orient started brightly and the unresponsive crowd was shaken from it's torpor as Scott McGleish rose to meet a Jimmy Smith flick-on to head past the Plymouth goalkeeper after only four minutes. Less than ten minutes later, Alex Revell raced clear and squared for Dean Cox to smash Orient into a two-goal lead that already looked to be insurmountable.

Not wanting to check the Spurs score until Orient were comfortable, I now felt happy enough to pull out my phone. Chas got there first, and with a laugh turned his screen to me to pass on the bad news. Spurs were a goal down and a man down after just fifteen minutes, Peter Crouch had been sent off after two bookings in quick succession. I groaned and slumped back in my seat. At least the O's were doing the business. It was already damage-limitation for Spurs against a very good team. I gave up hope almost immediately.

With Orient well on top, I grew increasingly attached to my phone, refreshing every few seconds for an update.

'Are you watching this game or not?' Jamie said, pointing at the action in front of me as if I hadn't noticed it.

Spurs survived the first half without conceding again, while Orient went into the break two goals up and playing such relaxed football it seemed likely Jamie Jones would reappear for the second half with a book to read.

Although the second half remained scoreless at Brisbane Road, Orient continued to dominate and Plymouth were just awful. Rooted to the foot of the table after a ten-point deduction for going into administration, they were playing as if they had already been relegated. Yet there was a decent turn out of away fans considering the distance from the south-west coast and the midweek kick-off. Players, managers and administrators can come and go, but the fans are a perpetual presence. Despite the dire performance and hopeless league position, the Plymouth fans were doing themselves proud.

In the Spanish capital, the Spurs faithful were being tested too. Real had gone up several gears and swept ten-man Tottenham aside 4-0. To add insult to injury, former Arsenal striker Emmanuel Adebayor scored two. Murph and Chas were revelling in the defeat and rubbing it in. I was endeavouring to rise above it and maintain composure.

'That's Spurs out of the Champions League then. Normal service resumed,' Chas crowed.

'How did you lot get on tonight?' I replied. 'Oh no, wait, you got knocked out in the previous round didn't you? Another trophyless season for Arsenal. Normal service resumed.'

I didn't usually get involved in the tit-for-tat petty squabbles between Arsenal and Spurs, but I was on strong ground on this one.

On the positive side, Orient gained three important points and although Rochdale also won, keeping them above us, sixth-place Bournemouth dropped more points and the chasing pack were snapping at their heels. The marathon was beginning to enter a sprint finish.

Saturday 9th April 2011
Orient v Southampton

If a marathon is the athletics equivalent of football league season, the horse-racing parallel has to be the Grand National – a big field, a long distance, glory to the winner. Being a low-key gambler, dabbling with the odd pound on football accumulators every so often, the Grand National is one of the few occasions I put any of my hard-earned cash on the nags. This year I stuck a fiver on Midnight Club and Can't Catch Time and drew BecauseICantSee in the office sweepstake.

With Jamie and his loose bowels in gay Paris, Cads took his place in Leyton. It was a baking hot day and my shorts and flip-flops were released from the dark corner of the wardrobe that they had occupied for the last six months. The bookies on Leyton High Road was packed with hopeful punters and to mark their biggest day of the year a small trestle table had been set up laden with crisps, nuts and soft drinks.

It was just as busy around the ground. Southampton brought plenty of support but there were noticeably more O's fans present and the Supporters Club was heaving inside and out. The effect a play-off push and a sunny day can have on attendances is remarkable.

Orient got off to a decent start and controlled play, but a sloppy piece of defending allowed the visitors to go a goal in front as Rickie Lambert nodded home at the near post.

'Oh for fuck's sake! Lambert!' Paul groaned behind us. 'He always scores against us! If Barnard gets one too, I think I might cry!'

Orient struggled to find an opening, but with the amount of possession we were getting, it was surely just a matter of time.

For the second match in a row, the Orient players on the pitch did not have my full attention. At 4:20 we turned our interest to the Grand National. Chas managed to get live BBC coverage on his phone and we craned our necks to get a decent view of the screen as the horses thundered around the course. A few fans who had money riding on the race began to turn to us for updates. Like inadequate versions of Sir Peter O'Sullevan, we attempted to recount what we were watching. By the time the final fences approached, two of my three horses had fallen and my last hope was a mile behind. I relaxed back into my seat after finding myself perched right on the edge of it.

Turning back to the thoroughbreds at Brisbane Road, the O's were playing some lovely stuff. Were it not for the linesman's flag, Jimmy Smith would have had a couple of goals. Luck had deserted me in the Grand National, but it couldn't avoid me completely. A breakthrough was coming, and it would be the least that Orient deserved.

Sometimes, what a team deserves and what a team gets is completely different. With just minutes to go, Paul's nightmare came true. Former Orient striker Lee Barnard grabbed Southampton's second goal. Cupping his ear, he ran at the supporters in the North Stand, who heaped abuse on him.

'Argh!' Paul groaned again behind us. 'Anyone but him, for fuck's sake!' Paul was proving to be a real clairvoyant. Maybe I would ask him for a Grand National bet next year.

The full-time disappointment was etched on our faces. After a quick beer in the Supporters Club we watched Lee Barnard get a bit more stick as he climbed aboard the Southampton team coach. Lady Luck may not have been with me at either Aintree or Brisbane Road, but she had seen fit for Rochdale and Bournemouth to lose, meaning the league remained as it was before kick-off. Thank heaven for small mercies.

Tuesday 12th April 2011
Orient v Carlisle United

The house purchase was still up in the air. We needed several different parties to sign off one small document, and everybody that mattered, it seemed, had gone on holiday. Stace and I were chasing our solicitor on a day-to-day basis for an update. We wanted to give notice on our flat, but it was looking increasingly likely we were staying put for at least another month.

For the second week in a row, Orient had a Tuesday match. The fixture list stacked up at the most important moment of the season. Both players and fans were weary. The absence of football in December was being made up for in April, and it was probably not doing our nerves and patience any good.

Jamie was back after posting a personal best 3 hour, 50 minute time in the Paris marathon. For someone who abuses his body on such a regular basis it has always amazed me that he is capable of completing a marathon, let alone doing it in under four hours.

'So how long is the Paris marathon?' Chas asked as we enjoyed a beer in the Supporters Club prior to kick-off.

'Err, it's a marathon, Chas,' Jamie said with a smirk.

'I thought they were different lengths?' he replied, looking confused.

'It's 26 miles you nob. It's always 26 miles. 26.22 to be exact. It's an official distance,' Jamie laughed as Chas frowned and stared thoughtfully into space, no nearer to being convinced.

Up in the stands, the crowd was muted again. Unlike Plymouth the week before, Carlisle had brought very few fans, making the whole stadium a morgue. The match did little to animate those who had turned up. It was scruffy and sloppy and Orient were struggling to find a rhythm. Tired defending allowed half-chances at both ends, but neither side could manage a decent finish.

Worryingly for the home support, Jamie Jones was the busier of the two keepers. He had been in excellent form all season despite a few shaky moments, but he picked tonight to show everyone why he should be destined for bigger and better things.

When people talk of super saves, Gordon Banks' stop against Brazil is often the top of the pile. It was bettered when Jones, wrong-footed by an effort on goal and drifting across his line in the wrong direction, jerked his body back the opposite way. As if possessed by Banks himself, an outstretched arm made it to the oncoming ball and flicked it around the post. The fans behind the goal had already accepted that Carlisle had scored, but as his palm turned the ball away from the gaping net, the outcry of delight and applause was such that a passer-by would think the home team had scored. For lower-league football naysayers, it is moments of magic like this that prove flashes of football genius are not confined to the top flight.

Mostly thanks to Jones, the game remained locked at 0-0 at half-time and the stalemate continued into the second half. It was a frustrating game for all concerned. Orient upped the tempo but were guilty of some profligacy in front of goal. Groans of despair emanated from every side of the ground.

With just five minutes left, Orient laid siege to the Carlisle goal. Adam Chambers missed a decent chance to win the game, then Dean Cox missed the best of all. M'Poku whipped an impeccable low cross with Cox rushing into the penalty area and the winger thrust his head at the ball. In front of an empty goal, just yards out, his header spooned up and over the bar. Cox was spread-eagled on the ground, aware he had missed a sitter. With a cry of anguish, my frustration boiled over and I whacked the seat in front of me, a knuckle cracking painfully on the unforgiving plastic.

The final whistle blew and the expressions on the faces of the crowd told the story. Two points dropped, and with Rochdale beating Southampton, a play-off place was now a long shot.

The following evening I watched a spirited and plucky Spurs lose 1-0 to Real Madrid in the second leg of the Champions League. Despite a host of good chances to salvage some pride in a tie that was beyond them, the only goal came at Spurs' end when a Gomes clanger settled the game. To make matters worse it was the smug, preening Cristiano Ronaldo that benefitted from the Spurs keeper's mistake.

My interest in the Premier League had waned considerably as the season had progressed, mainly because watching Orient had taken up such a large portion of my attention. Spurs' participation in Europe had brought some welcome variety, but they eventually succumbed to the might and wealth of Real Madrid and were out of the Champions League. It looked like being a single-season experience too. Spurs were largely out of the running for fourth place in the Premier League and the Champions League qualifying spot as Manchester City's billions were bearing fruit. Spurs were hardly paupers, but financial clout was having its say in the Champions League and the Premier League as usual.

I was glad I had Orient. Promotion was unlikely, but being as close to it as they were was a remarkable achievement. They were there on merit and merit alone, not by buying their way. Whatever the coming games brought, it was something I was proud to be a part of.

With Orient away at Exeter, I spent the entire Saturday in front of Jeff Stelling and his *Soccer Saturday* team. From being an incessant viewer a few months previously, for the last month I had paid little attention to Sky's relentless football news coverage.

The O's got off to a shoddy start, conceding after just four minutes, but Dean Cox levelled things up soon after with a screamer from 25 yards. At this stage in the season every point was vital, so a draw away at Exeter wouldn't have been a bad result. Even better, Rochdale and Bournemouth were drawing too. At this time of the season football fans become mini-mathmeticians, calculating various permutations of the ever-changing league table at a moment's notice. As it stood, just two points separated Orient in eighth and Rochdale in sixth, the all-important last play-off place.

If the forecast was fair at half-time, by full-time the clouds had gathered and there were rumbles of thunder in the distance. Exeter grabbed a winner midway through the second half, bringing them level with us on points, while Bournemouth grabbed two goals to take all three points away at Notts County. It was small consolation that Rochdale succumbed to a late goal at home to Brentford, because now five points lay between Orient and the play-offs. With four games remaining, the gap looked a wide one.

It was awards week in the football community. Tottenham winger Gareth Bale was crowned PFA Footballer of the Year, a strange decision given that he had a patchy season in the Premier League, although his performances in the Champions League drew praise from all corners of Europe. What was more surprising was that no Orient players had made the League One team of the season. The O's left-sided combination of Charlie Daniels and Dean Cox had the most goals and assists in the entire country, yet they were overlooked in favour of higher-profile names from Southampton, Huddersfield and Brighton. Perhaps even in the lower leagues bigger teams still carry the weight of favour.

<u>Friday 22nd April 2011</u>
<u>Orient v Peterborough United</u>

Orient's next home game against Peterborough United was a must win. With Easter and Prince William and Kate Middleton's royal wedding, Good Friday marked the first of four bank holidays over the coming days. The country was planning a good old knees-up, but Orient needed to concentrate on the task in hand.

Many chose to take a few days off to extend the holiday, including Calum, the 18-year-old boyfriend of Murph's sister. Murph, a protective older brother, invited Calum to Brisbane Road while he was down from Middlesbrough for the Easter holidays. It was a getting-to-know-you exercise which allowed him to run the rule over his sister's would-be suitor.

Ten years our junior, Calum was quiet at first, but he kept up with us pint-for-pint and got into the swing of things quick enough once he'd figured out we weren't going to bite him. We were testing our recall of random football trivia facts and soon got into naming brothers who have played in the Premier League.

'The Nevilles,' Chas offered.

'Jerome and Kevin-Prince Boateng,' Murph added.

'Shaun and Bradley Wright-Phillips,' Joss suggested, to nods of agreement.

'How about Rod and Danny Wallace?' I ventured.

'Who are they?' Calum asked.

'Danny and Rod Wallace? You've never heard them? Are you kidding?' I said bemused, before realising that at 18 years of age, young Calum would have spent the best part of the Wallaces' career in nappies. Football moves fast, and at that moment I felt very old.

A good crowd filled the stands; the bank holiday was clearly having a positive effect on the attendance. The Peterborough fans were in good voice. They were guaranteed a play-off place and were clearly enjoying the sunshine, an extended season already assured. Hopefully the Posh players would be equally laid back, we needed three points a lot more than they did.

The game was open and scrappy with a few tasty but fair challenges flying in, and the ref had a mad five minutes during which he showed yellow cards for the slightest infringement. By half-time there had been few clear-cut chances and 0-0 was about right on the balance of play.

In spite of the heat, the second half took off at pace and Orient soon took the lead from an unlikely source. Stephen Dawson, put through on the left, raced towards the byline. Seeing Alex Revell in the box, he squared it, only for the retreating figure of former O's centre-back Gabriel Zakuani to turn the ball past his own keeper. The Tommy Johnston Stand erupted into chants of 'once a blue, always a red' as Zakuani, looking bashful having helped out his old team, picked himself up and walked slowly back to his position.

The lead didn't last long, Orient conceded a soft goal eight minutes later. They failed to deal with a set piece and a Posh substitute fresh from the bench beat his marker and headed deep into the corner past Jamie Jones. It was deflating. A draw simply wasn't good enough.

Slade made his last roll of the dice, throwing on fringe player Ryan Jarvis who had barely played all season. With few chances created in the final ten minutes, the game moved into added time. If Sir Alex Ferguson has a knack of influencing stoppage time in the Premier League when the game is close, then his son Darren, manager of Peterborough, has the same effect. An extra six minutes were signalled by the fourth official.

Ferguson may have held out hopes for a win, but in the 96th minute it was Orient's Jason Crowe who picked up the ball on the left hand side. Striding into space, he looked up and curled a beautifully flighted cross to the far post where Ryan Jarvis was waiting. Jarvis leapt, leaning all over his marker, and directed the ball into the net. The crowd roared with delight, Jarvis spun away to celebrate, I waited for the official to disallow it for a foul. The referee thought that Jarvis' challenge was fine though, and called time for a 2-1 Orient victory. With three points in the bag, we now had to hope and pray that Carlisle and Yeovil would do us a favour tomorrow and take points off our promotion rivals.

We hit the Supporters Club for a celebratory drink or two then continued on to Wanstead. Calum still kept up with the drinking but was now a little hammered, but not as much as Chas who, after an extensive round of drinking games, fell off his bar stool and drenched himself in beer.

It was with a hangover that I followed *Soccer Saturday* the next day. At half-time, Bournemouth were two-up away at Yeovil and Rochdale were a goal down at home to Carlisle. We needed both to drop points. Yeovil managed to pull a goal back, but at almost the same time Rochdale scored two. Now both Bournemouth and Rochdale were 2-1 up.

A Carlisle equaliser came at almost the same instant as Jermian Defoe scored his hundredth goal for Spurs, putting them a goal up against West Brom. I cheered and punched the air, and it wasn't because Spurs had taken the lead. As final whistles blew up and down the country, there was still more drama to come. News flashed in from Huish Park that Yeovil had equalised against Bournemouth. Now both Bournemouth and Rochdale were drawing 2-2. Even better was to come. Jeff Stelling's excited voice froze me to the couch. 'There's been a fifth goal at Spotland!' Dean Windass' flustered face appeared on screen. 'Incredible Jeff, it's 3-2 and Carlisle have stolen it!'

'Yeeeees!' I screamed, leaping off the sofa. It was a lifeline from the heavens. Had Bournemouth and Rochdale kept their leads, Jarvis' late winner the day before would have merely prolonged the status quo. As it was, we took a big step towards the two teams ahead. Just three points separated us from the final play-off spot with three games left.

The exhausting schedule continued on Easter Monday, but I couldn't spend another day slouched on my backside at home. I'd promised to buy Stacey a handbag for her birthday and she called in the treat, meaning an afternoon traipsing around the shops of Covent Garden and Oxford Street on a sunny day. Fortunately, Stace hates shopping almost as much as I do and within five minutes the present was paid for, my duty as a boyfriend was done and we went for lunch. We whiled the rest of the afternoon away dodging tourists and wandering leisurely around the West End, Stace striding ahead while I sauntered behind, eyes fixed on my phone for score updates.

An Easter miracle was under way, Orient were being resurrected. Bournemouth were a goal down against relegation strugglers Bristol Rovers, Rochdale were losing against Charlton and Jonathan Téhoué had scored for the O's at Carlisle. I was planning the next couple of weeks already. If Orient were still in with a shout of the play-offs after Saturday's match against Tranmere, I would travel to Plymouth for the crucial final match of the season.

I locked on the scores, visualising every kick and every moment. Bristol Rovers were reduced to ten men, then Bournemouth were down to ten too. Must be a bad-tempered match. Rochdale grabbed an equaliser – nooo – but within minutes were behind again – yes! Orient clung to Téhoué's first half goal, inching closer to three points.

Then Bournemouth equalised. Four minutes later, they took the lead. Rochdale went down to a 2-1 loss, but Bournemouth's win was confirmed. Orient played on.

While we were waiting to catch the Number 8 bus back to Shoreditch, Orient conceded a penalty. Swearing loudly, startling an elderly lady and earning an elbow in the ribs from Stace, I refreshed frantically. Jamie Jones was injured, so reserve goalkeeper Lee Butcher was the man responsible for keeping Orient in the play-off hunt. Refresh. Refresh. Refresh. Butcher saves! With a thumping heart, wiping the sweat from my brow, I checked the league tables. Orient were in seventh and trailing Bournemouth by three points. MK Dons slipped up against Plymouth, so they were now only one point ahead of the Cherries in fifth. Rochdale trailed three points behind

Orient in eighth, out of contention after two defeats over the long Easter weekend.

In two matches over four days, Orient's chances had been significantly improved by perennial substitute Téhoué, reserve goalkeeper Butcher and outcast Ryan Jarvis. Improbable sources had made the most unlikely outcome a real possibility.

Every match was equally crucial now, but like George Orwell's pigs, Saturday's final home game was surely more equal than the others. I ran through every scenario possible, but whatever happened, we surely had to beat Tranmere at Brisbane Road. Notts County and Hartlepool could do Orient a huge favour, but three points against the team from the Wirral were critical.

Spurs' Champions League vanquishers, Real Madrid, faced their bitter rivals Barcelona in the semi-final. Although Tottenham's exit from the Champions League was a disappointment, it was a small consolation to know that if they had got past Real, they were likely to be humiliated and torn to shreds by the *tiki-taka* passing of the Catalan giants. Any meeting between these two heavyweights is given top billing by the sports media across Europe, and with the breadth of talent on the pitch it should have been a game to savour. Sadly for the watching world, *El Clásico* descended into farce as both sides tried to out-cheat the other: diving, petulant kicking, limp-wristed fisticuffs, pushing and shoving and very little football. Had it not been for Lionel Messi scoring a wonderous solo goal, the game would not have looked out of place in the Sunday

League. If this was the pinnacle of competitive club football, they could keep it.

The day of the royal wedding and another bank holiday arrived. Tacky wedding merchandise filled shop fronts across the kingdom, the streets were bedecked with bunting and Union flags. We joined a large group of friends and the rest of the festive throng in Hyde Park on a grey and overcast day. We cracked open the bubbly at 9 o'clock and by the time the service started at 11 we, along with most of the park, were well-oiled. As a proud Brit it was great to see so many people coming together in good spirits to celebrate as a nation. It was the first time I'd seen a royal wedding of any significance, and if all of them have the frivolity (and the day off) that this one had, I can't wait for the next one.

As Hyde Park looked on under a blanket of cloud, Kate Middleton glided majestically down the length of Westminster Abbey and the young Prince turned to her as she approached. The moment she joined his side, the cloud parted above us and a shaft of brilliant light burst through, bathing the park in sunshine to cheers from the enchanted crowd. It was a magical moment, never to be repeated.

The rest of the day was spent drinking in the sunshine. London, Britain and perhaps the world was in a very good mood.

Saturday 30th April 2011
Orient v Tranmere Rovers

If Friday was a big day for Britain, Saturday was an enormous one for Orient. Not only was it make or break for the play-offs, it was the last home game of the season and our final journey to Brisbane Road, virtually nine months since we walked through the turnstiles for the first time as season ticket holders.

Slightly hungover after the biggest wedding reception of all time, Jamie and I arrived at the Supporters Club so early that the opposition team coach was yet to arrive. Murph, Chas and Joss were waiting for us with a glint of eager anticipation in their eyes. Home and away supporters mingled amicably in the Supporters Club for hours before the game. The absence of animosity between Orient and almost all other fans in the football league had been one of the season's highlights. Friendly banter is all football fans should ever enjoy. There is no need to take things any further, and so far this season I'd barely witnessed a crossed word.

With fifteen minutes to kick-off we were in our seats, belting out the full repertoire of Orient songs while blowing up bright red balloons that Paul and his mates had brought to mark the occasion. Orient's cheerleaders, The Cheery O's, were dancing in the sunshine to Lady Gaga and continued to do so even when the sprinklers burst into life, much to the enjoyment of every male in attendance.

A cacophonous roar signalled the players taking to the field and we launched our balloons into the sky. The effect would have been great had a prevailing wind not caught them the instant they were released, forcing them to drift into a far corner of the Tommy Johnston Stand.

Orient settled into a good rhythm and the crowd were in full voice. Then disaster struck. Tranmere full-back Aaron Cresswell picked the ball up on the halfway line and moved unopposed into the Orient half. 35 yards from goal, he unleashed a rasping drive that beat a despairing dive from Jamie Jones and flew into the top corner. It was a magnificent strike, a haymaker punch that knocked the stuffing out of the entire ground.

The Orient players suddenly looked nervous. Perhaps news filtered to them that Bournemouth had also taken the lead. The afternoon could not have started worse. With steely determination, Orient knuckled down to the job at hand and began to dictate play. Creating only half-chances but defending resolutely, they pressed the visitors into their own half as the match approached the interval. Then Matt Spring, usually composed, fell victim to a moment of madness.

Under no pressure, in the centre of the park, he lay a lazy and under-hit pass across the field into the path of Tranmere's Adam McGurk. The Rovers striker surged forward, no Orient defender close to him, and curled a perfect shot past Jones to make it 2-0.

We took stock. We were two down, Bournemouth two up and now MK Dons were a goal ahead too. It was over.

Orient were choking, and they knew it. Heads went down on and off the pitch. The body language of the players betrayed their lack of confidence. After an exhausting run of fixtures – this was their eighth match in April – they had little energy remaining and a two-goal deficit was a mountain to climb.

The crowd sang loud, a vain, desperate attempt to breathe life into the players, but Tranmere delivered the coup de grâce five minutes into the second half. Cresswell smashed a free kick across the penalty area and McGurk chested the ball over the line. 3-0. Game over, season over.

22 players went through the motions. Tranmere were happy to allow Orient to have the ball, safe in the knowledge that they were a beaten team. It was a limp end to the season.

Tempers were fraught in the stand and tensions bubbled over behind us. One fan, who had amused us all season by shouting pointless and useless advice to the players at inappropriate moments, offered some typical words of wisdom. 'In the box!' he shouted, despite Orient being in their own half.

One young chap lost his rag after hearing the same banal phrase for the thousandth time. 'Why don't you fuck off you cunt!' he shouted angrily. 'You're a fucking joke!'

Rather than 'in the box' taking offence, it was a middle-aged man next to him who rose to his feet and approached the youngster, giving him a volley of verbals and threatening him. The young chap returned some abuse. Some pushing and shoving started and several bystanders stood up to block the warring factions from engaging each other.

Trouble in the stands at Orient? This was unprecedented. Fueled by frustration and disappointment at the wilting of a season that promised so much, fellow O's had turned on each other.

A burly member of the security team climbed the stairs towards the arguing parties. On seeing the high-visibility jacket heading their way, both tried their best to look innocent, like naughty youngsters caught being mischeavious in the school playground.

'Are we all being nice to each other?' the security man asked with raised eyebrows and a knowing smile. His laid-back manner raised some laughs and defused the situation perfectly. The warring factions returned to their seats ruefully to see out the rest of the game.

At full-time the players disappeared down the tunnel, but they quickly re-emerged for a circuit of the pitch to rapturous applause. They may have been well beaten, but the season as a whole had been magnificent. The football they played did the club and the division proud. It had been far from smooth sailing – a patchy start cost valuable points that would have made all the difference at the end of the season – but overall, Orient had punched above their weight.

The players still had a long trip to Plymouth to endure before the season ended properly, but this marked the end of our journey. Geographically we had only gone as far as

Norfolk, but on the road to becoming committed Orient fans we had gone much further.

We slowly, reluctantly made our way down the steps of the stand and through the open gate emptying fans onto Buckingham Road. What the bloody hell was I going to do with my Saturdays now?

Players mingled with fans in the Supporters Club, commiserating, celebrating and congratulating. We accosted Dean Cox and Scott McGleish for a quick photo and they were only too happy to oblige.

'Don't get too drunk now lads,' McGleish said with a smile. Turning on his heels, he left the bar and disappeared from sight. We made no promises.

```
 4.Peterborough United.P45|W22|D10|L13|F101A75|76pts
 5.MK Dons.............P45|W22|D8 |L15|F65|A59|74pts
 6.Bournemouth........P45|W19|D14|L12|F74|A52|71pts
 7.Leyton Orient......P45|W18|D13|L14|F67|A61|67pts
 8.Exeter.............P45|W19|D10|L16|F64|A72|67pts
 9.Rochdale...........P45|W17|D14|L14|F61|A54|65pts
10.Brentford..........P45|W17|D9 |L19|F51|A58|60pts
```

May 2011

The loose threads of a long and eventful season were being pulled together, neatened and trimmed to size. Clubs across all leagues were jostling for position, some with eyes on promotion and others facing the grim spectre of relegation.

Manchester City reached the final of the FA Cup at the expense of Manchester United, the club from whose shadow they were beginning to emerge, albeit with serious financial help. United were still happy though, three points ahead of Chelsea at the top of the Premier League with three games remaining and with a forthcoming Champions League final against Barcelona.

Spurs, after their own Champions League adventure, were seven points from fourth place and it would be almost impossible for them to make an instant return to the competition they had lit up so brightly. City's extensive spending had brought returns and they looked certain to take Tottenham's place in next season's Champions League.

Orient, having got so close, couldn't drag themselves over the line when it mattered and an insurmountable four-point gap lay between them and the play-offs with just one game left. All that remained was to play for pride, and after the season they'd had, pride was something they had accumulated in abundance.

The disappointment of the end of the season was lifted by the news that our house worries were at an end. The checks were complete, the mortgage offer arranged, the deposit was resting in my account and waiting for the green light. The contract exchange was arranged for 16th May with the moving day a month later.

Cardboard boxes were beginning to pile up, floor to ceiling, in our tiny flat. Having shuttled backwards and forwards down the Central Line so often over the previous nine months, in a little over four weeks we would be living a mere ten-minute walk from Brisbane Road. I knew there was a chance that my heart would find a home in Leyton after a season watching Orient. That the rest of me would find one too was a development I had not foreseen.

Having spent an entire season consuming beer, hot dogs and pies and watching other people exert themselves on a Saturday afternoon, we decided it was time we put ourselves through our paces. Instead of the trip to Plymouth I'd promised myself if Orient beat Tranmere, Chas, Murph and I dragged our out-of-shape torsos to Wanstead Leisure Centre for a game of badminton. Portsmouth fan Phil joined us, having endured a rollercoaster season that put the combined travails of Orient and Spurs to shame. Phil, who lives in South Woodford, is a regular at Fratton Park and clocked up an incredible number of miles over the course of the season.

As we dashed around the court, flailing wildly at the shuttlecock as it looped back and forth, we kept a close eye on the Orient score. They went into an early two-goal lead through McGleish and Cox and seemed to be condemning already-relegated Plymouth to a miserable end to the season.

By the time we finished our session the full-time scores were coming in. Although Plymouth had pulled a goal back, two late goals from Alex Revell capped off a fine 4-1 win for Orient. Bournemouth, already safe in the play-offs, lost at home to Rochdale. It meant that Orient missed out on the play-offs by just a single point.

It was an agonisingly small margin. When such things happen, it is almost impossible not to look back at points dropped over the season. Tranmere and Yeovil at home in the final month were the most recent guilty moments, but only taking a point from two games against relegated Dagenham and Redbridge also cost us dear.

But luck goes both ways. Orient had claimed more than their fair share of last-minute draws and winners.

Bournemouth, Peterborough and Oldham at home, Huddersfield away, the late goals all contributed to a points haul that took the O's to within a whisker of the play-offs.

The league table never lies. For all the unbeaten runs, last-gasp winners and lucky points on the road, Orient's whole season was built on a solid foundation of defeats. The momentum the team gathered after the New Year almost, but not quite, wiped away the abysmal start. Had the league campaign started better, had they won one of their first three home games, had they had the services of Paul-Jose M'Poku, Tom Carroll and Harry Kane from the first match, who knows where they would be now?

But that is football. A collection of ifs, buts, could-haves and would-haves. And a league table that can't be altered.

Brighton and Southampton were promoted. Huddersfield, Peterborough, MK Dons and Bournemouth were set for a slightly longer season as play-off contenders. At the other end of the table, Dagenham and Redbridge and Plymouth were joined by Bristol Rovers and Swindon in dropping to League Two. Relegation is a bitter pill to swallow for any team, but Plymouth would feel even worse. While Manchester City and their bottomless pit of money were scaling the heights of the Premier League and participating in the FA Cup final, Plymouth, with no money at all, were deducted ten points for going into administration. Those ten points were the difference between the safety of nineteenth position and their eventual fate of 23rd. Football's haves and have-nots were never so clearly defined.

The season over, the concern for Orient fans turned to holding on to their best players. During the week, goalkeeper Jamie Jones had amended his Twitter profile from 'Goalkeeper for Leyton Orient' to 'League One goalkeeper'. This sparked a flurry of worried messages from O's fans speculating on what it could mean.

There was no doubt that Jones was worthy of elevation to a bigger club. His performances throughout the season were excellent, and at the age of 22 he surely was destined for greener pastures beyond Brisbane Road. As a Spurs fan, I was used to having our best players plucked from us by Manchester United or Arsenal fighting it out at the top of the league, but Orient, with a shoe-string budget, were open to all comers. Jones was just one of a number of players who could happily ply their trade in the Championship. Like a rotting carcass on the plains of Africa, we were at the mercy of large, strong scavenging clubs who could pick our bones clean. Russell Slade faced a huge challenge assembling and motivating a team good enough to reach the fifth round of the FA Cup and to finish seventh in the league. Now he faced a bigger challenge holding on to the team he had created.

Sweating from my exertions on the badminton court, I arrived home in time to watch Spurs take on Blackpool. I had all but given up on any chance of Tottenham returning to the Champions League, but Manchester City had lost to Everton and with the two sides meeting in the week, a replay of last season's unofficial fourth-place decider, we were still mathematically in with a shout.

A season watching Orient had cooled my temper when watching Spurs, but it threatened to return when they turned out a terrible performance against a side who were flirting with relegation. It took a late equaliser from Jermain Defoe to rescue a point after Charlie Adam, lucky to be on the pitch following a savage challenge on Gareth Bale, tucked a penalty away late in the second half.

Spurs' only chance was to beat Manchester City at Eastlands, but in an act of bitter irony, Peter Crouch, who struck with such devastating effect in the same fixture a year before to clinch fourth place, scored the only goal of the game again – past his own goalkeeper. The game finished 1-0 to City and secured their first participation in the Champions League.

My football viewing was over for another season. Nearly. I still had one more game to see.

Murph's stag-do was a good reason to continue our European football tour. We were off to Barcelona and had tickets to Barca's final league game of the season against Deportivo La Coruña. Having already wrapped up the league title and with a Champions League final to come, Barca were not likely to field a full-strength side. But even their reserve team has players that could find their way into the first team at Old Trafford, the Emirates or Stamford Bridge, so we still expected some razzle-dazzle at the Camp Nou.

As stag-dos go, it wasn't the raucous, no-holds-barred trip that gives stag-dos a bad reputation. While we wanted to have a good time, we knew Murph was not one for being ritually humiliated or force-fed tequila from his own shoe, so we were going to take it easy on him. Not that we told Murph that. If he expected us to strip him naked and leave him stranded on Las Ramblas, we decided the fear of such torment probably outweighed the act itself.

The drinking was as full-on as expected, the nights as long and late as we could make them and we had a good old time. We caught the FA Cup final in a bar just off Las Ramblas and, as expected, Man City lifted the famous trophy after a 1-0 win over Stoke City. It was far from a classic and we spent most of the game reminiscing about finals of old. It was nice to see a different team winning the competition, but it felt like City had paid for the trophy in advance.

We wandered around like zombies on the day of the match at Camp Nou having endured two days and nights of boozing. Although Murph had escaped real punishment, we couldn't allow him to get away with it entirely. He dressed for the day as a Barcelona über-fan, costumed in a full Barcelona kit, blue-and-maroon jester's hat, a Catalan flag tied round his waist like a skirt and blue-and-maroon face paint. On the back of the shirt, in bright yellow lettering, was a number 4 and 'Fabregas' emblazoned across the top. With the Catalans courting Arsenal's captain for the past two-and-a-half seasons, it seemed inevitable that Fabregas would eventually make the move over the summer. It was a calculated insult to Arsenal-fan Murph.

'Oooh, that's low!' Murph groaned with a wry smile as we held the shirt in front of him. 'I can't believe you let them do that, Chas!'

Wandering the streets looking like a complete berk, eliciting howls of laughter from passers-by and posing for photos for those brave enough to approach, we bundled Murph into a taxi and made our way to the stadium.

Outside, Barca flags waved and thousands of blue-and-maroon fans chatted and laughed in clusters. We mingled with them, enjoying cans of beer bought from street side vendors for just €1.

Once inside, we climbed the steps high into the stadium. Our seats were located on the back row, just in front of one of the giant screens that loom over the goals at either end of the famous ground. The views were staggering. The hillside rose high in the distance behind the opposite end and the landscape darkened slowly as the sun set to our left. We looked down on a cauldron of colour whose beautifully curved sides swept majestically around on either side of us. The 80,000 fans gathered below us filled the air with noise as the teams filed out like two lines of ants from the tunnel.

The game didn't live up to the setting. With bigger fish to fry at Wembley in a fortnight, a predictably low-key Barcelona side took to the field. They kept the ball as well as their regular eleven, but the thrust and cutting-edge that players like David Villa, Xavi Hernandez, Andres Iniesta and Lionel Messi usually provided was missing.

By the time the final whistle blew, ending the game 0-0, darkness had fully descended and the illuminated expanse of pitch was all that was visible, as if floating gently through the blackness of space.

The players were joined by their rested team mates in a lap of honour, clutching La Liga trophy as fireworks lit up the sky and confetti rained down onto the pitch. Having watched Orient's lap of honour a couple of weeks before, it was incredible to think that the same sport brought this kind of tumultuous celebration. The size and stature of a club like Barcelona is hard to comprehend. The players below us were treated like gods and millions of fans around the world were celebrating their achievements. Orient were lucky to get a few thousand to Brisbane Road. It was a different world.

Seven tired and broken men entered Barcelona airport and joined the queue to check in. Not realising the time, we dashed for the departure gate tugging our cases behind us. As we approached the gate my phone began vibrating in my pocket. It was Dave, my solicitor.

'Hi Adam, can you talk?' he asked.

'I'm just about to get on a plane, can it wait?'

'I'm just calling to say we are ready to exchange contracts on the house. I just need your approval to release the funds and you're done.'

'Blimey!' I said laughing. This was a surreal moment. 'You have my permission to proceed,' I said, feigning an officious voice.

'Excellent, congratulations, you've just bought a house in Leyton.'

Back in England, the final games of the season were played out. Spurs secured fifth place beating Birmingham 2-1, condemning their opponents to relegation. Man City clinched third in the Premier League, and with it, automatic qualification into the Champions League to go along with their FA Cup victory. Arsenal capitulated in their final games and a draw against Fulham in the last match of the season dropped them down to fourth.

UEFA's showpiece Champions League final at Wembley was high on hype and low on delivery. The meeting of the champions of the two best leagues in the world should have been a game for the ages but Barcelona once again outclassed Manchester United, just as they had two years before. The 3-1 scoreline didn't reflect the dominance Barcelona exerted on their English opponents, and for the fourth time in their history, the European Cup was going back to Camp Nou.

In League One, Peterborough surprised everybody, except perhaps themselves, by beating Huddersfield convincingly in the play-off final to claim promotion to the Championship. Tumbling down in the opposite direction to face Orient next season were Sheffield United, Preston North End and Scunthorpe United.

As the sun set on the season, we were already anticipating the dawn of the next one. With a few canny additions Orient could well push on and make the play-offs, perhaps more. Russell Slade vowed to keep many of Orient's best players at the club, a promotion push was being mooted and the decision to award West Ham the right to occupy the now fully-built Olympic Stadium had been overturned pending a Judicial Review.

Jamie, Chas, Murph, Joss and I had renewed our season tickets. As I was moving just a stone's throw from the ground it would be silly not to, but the decision was made long before the season had ended and the house contracts exchanged. It wasn't one singular moment that clinched it in a road-to-Damascus revelation. Not the big win against Sheffield Wednesday, the away day at Norwich or the delight of the last-minute equaliser against Arsenal. It was the feeling we got every time we knew we were off to watch the O's. It was the coming together, the beers, the laughs and the collective enjoyment of the game. My love of the game had been reignited.

```
 4.Peterborough United.P46|W23|D10|L13|F106A75|79pts
 5.MK Dons.............P46|W23|D8 |L15|F67|A60|77pts
 6.Bournemouth.........P46|W19|D14|L13|F75|A54|71pts
 7.Leyton Orient.......P46|W19|D13|L14|F71|A62|70pts
 8.Exeter..............P46|W20|D10|L16|F66|A73|70pts
 9.Rochdale............P46|W18|D14|L14|F63|A55|68pts
10.Colchester United...P46|W16|D14|L16|F57|A63|62pts
```

Epilogue

The vidiprinter flashed up the latest scoreline from Brunton Park. Carlisle netted a fourth unanswered goal and the game was all but over at half-time. Orient were on course for their tenth league defeat of the season. Sighing and rolling my eyes in resignation, I continued to untangle the string of fairy lights from the now sparsely-covered branches of our Christmas tree. It was almost a year to the day that we had followed the O's to East Anglia for the FA Cup victory over Norwich. Times had changed.

Over the summer, Stace and I left our tiny shoebox of a flat and settled into a home of our very own. Nestled on the boundary of Leyton and Leytonstone, our upstairs late Victorian maisonette is just a long goal kick away from Brisbane Road. Convincing Stace that this area was the place to settle will forever rank as one of my finest achievements.

Pre-season optimism quickly evaporated. Five successive defeats saw Orient glued to the foot of the table and it wasn't until October that they were able to secure a league win. Despite Slade's promises, the team that had enjoyed success in the previous season was beginning to break up. Jamie Jones was in the treatment room, the strike partnership of Scott McGleish and Alex Revell both left for pastures new, right-back Elliot Omuzusi was imprisoned for two-and-a-half years. Charlie Daniels and Stephen Dawson legged it during the January transfer window, finding more lucrative contracts elsewhere.

It is a fact of life for many smaller clubs in the lower leagues. Without serious financial input, clubs will remain in a constant state of flux. Teams can be constructed and can crumble within the space of months. Clubs whose revenues straddle the knife-edge between red and black are forced to find funds wherever and whenever they can. Offers for players are often, for the sake of the club's future, too good to refuse.

This perpetual treading of water will condemn Orient to an eternity of flitting between moderately good and horrifically bad seasons. The good may see a cup run, a play-off push or even promotion. The bad will involve the club stranded in the bottom half of the table fighting relegation.

Where do I stand in all of this? I have willingly aligned myself to a club bereft of success and with economic stability far from certain. What has it achieved in my life as a follower of football? The short answer, bizarrely, is that I'm happier.

I only ever set out to enjoy regular football with friends on a Saturday afternoon, something that from being a small boy, I was not able to do. What I actually experienced was more than I expected. I was no longer looking at football through a TV screen. I was up close and personal, not just with the fans around me, but also the players, the manager and the chairman.

The cynical may accuse me of breaking a golden rule in football – switching from supporting one club to another. Let me be 100% clear. I am still a Tottenham Hotspur supporter. I will continue to shout and swear at the TV screen whenever Tottenham play, and I look forward to the occasional times when I get the chance to go to White Hart Lane to watch a match.

Something has changed, however. My eyes have been opened to the opportunity of enjoying football as it should be. Free from hyperbole, free from media overexposure, free from over-pricing. I can now go with friends, sit with them and enjoy the collective human experience that football should be. There are no pretensions, no hang-ups and no animosity. Sometimes the football is bad, occasionally the refs are appalling and often (very often this season) results don't go our way. It's all part of the fun.

Leyton Orient prides itself as a club at the centre of a community. It is that spirit of community that gives Orient its warmth. After just one season, I feel a connection to the club that will remain a permanent part of my life. Murph, Chas, Jamie and Joss feel the same. We now share a constant in our lives, a fixed point of reference.

Good friends though we are, we will inevitably see less of each other as we get older. Everyone has their own path to tread. Murph got hitched, founded a company, disbanded a company, moved back to Essex and has now returned to banking. Jamie continues to party hard, but has found himself a nice girl to party with monogamously. Chas has his sights on working in the States in the near future. Joss will soon become a dad for the first time. I am now engaged and will be spending the next year of my life planning a wedding (football was clearly not that much of an impediment for Stace after all). We're all busy people with busy lives, but on Saturday afternoon our compass needles will now always point to Brisbane Road.

Acknowledgements

This book has been a pleasure to write and amassing the material and memories that have gone into it would not have been possible without my four South Stand companions: Anthony Murphy, Charles Wilman, Jamie Fleming and Jonathan 'Joss' Helme. Your company at matches is always a pleasure and the encouragement you gave me once I got my head down and started writing was a source of real motivation.

I'd also like to thank the supporters of Leyton Orient football club. The passion and pride you have in your club is matched by the warmth of your welcome. I'll see you in the Supporters Club soon for a crisp, golden pint of ale or two.

My sister Karen deserves a huge pat on the back for agreeing to read through the entire manuscript. Even with a part-time job and two young kids snapping at your heels 24 hours a day, you still found time to read through the meandering and at times foul-mouthed thoughts of your little brother. For that I thank you muchly!

Thanks to John Crace for reviewing the book and providing it with a fantastic cover quote. As a fellow Spurs supporter and long-suffering football fan in general, it was reassuring to receive such a positive response from someone with the gravitas and experience that he has.

A big thanks to Scott Reeves and everyone involved at Chequered Flag Publishing: Ivan Cartwright-Terry, Matt Conroy, Steve Coyle, Gary Reeves and Roisin Reeves. It was a bit of whirlwind getting everything together to complete the book in time but you were incredibly help-ful and hugely supportive.

Lastly, the biggest thanks of all go to my future wife Stacey. You've put up with my football fanaticism from day one and stayed with me despite the moods, the shout-ing, the ranting and the swearing. You were a constant source of support during the writing of the book and your belief that I wasn't wasting my time really focused my efforts and got me over the line.

Chequered Flag
PUBLISHING

www.chequeredflagpublishing.co.uk